THE
HEART
of the
FATHER

JOS   RODRIGUEZ

What People Are Saying About The Heart of The Father...........

"In these difficult times where the need for the hearts of fathers in our families and society intensifies, God is raising men and women to instruct and model the heart of our Father God to the world. Through this book, Pastor Joshua Rodríguez reveals answers from God to many questions in relation to the family, integration into the church and into the world. It is a publication that emerges in times of emergency! Entering into these pages will change your perspective of who God is. He will heal your soul and redeem your Christian doctrine."

Apostle Marlyn Arroyo Hernández

"*The Heart of the Father* is a book that reminds us of the unconditional love of God and gives us a new perspective of what true paternity is. In a time when the disintegration of the family is more alarming each day due to the absence of true paternal leadership, the book *The Heart of the Father*, written by Pastor Joshua Rodríguez, is without a doubt a useful tool to restore and equip the family to fulfill God's purposes."

Juan A. Sariñana, Senior Pastor
Iglesia Centro Evangelistico Ebenezer, Cudahy, California

Dedication

This book is dedicated to my father, Justino Rodríguez Quiñones, for his example and model of integrity, loyalty and commitment. To my father-in-law and second father, Pascual Acosta Ramírez, for teaching me to dedicate myself to maintaining my family united at all times. To my brother, Rev. David Rodriguez Falero, for teaching me to grow and stand out in life. To my spiritual father, Rev. Domingo Rodríguez Díaz, for having given birth to me in the faith and for imparting in me a spirit of integrity.

Acknowledgements

———— ∞∞∞ ————

I want to thank my beloved wife Paula for her patience with me and for stretching me so that I can develop one hundred percent of my gifts, talents, and abilities. To my four children, Joshua, Timothy, Gabriella, and Daniella for being such obedient and understanding children with the demands of our calling as a priestly family.

To the hundreds of spiritual sons and daughters that I have the honor to pastor as part of the Cityline Church family and to my transcription team: Grace Jimenez, Sabrina Rosario, Aury Masa-Nuñez, Elias Rodriguez, and Michelle Motta.

To the men of God that through the years, have imparted gifts and grace over my life and have offered their friendship, fellowship, and mentorship: Pastor Luciano Padilla Jr., Dr. Luís Carlo, Pastor Juan Antonio Sariñana, Pastor Roberto Candelario, Pastor Javier Vélez, Pastor David Greco, Pastor Radhames Fernández, Pastor Salvador Sabino, Pastor Frank Almonte, Pastor Jorge Roa Jr., Pastor Daniel Bonilla, Dr. Marcos Rivera, Dr. Pablo Díaz, Dr. Ender Vargas, Dr. Bob Nichols, Pastor Basilio Patiño, Dr. A.R. Bernard and Evangelist Nicky Cruz.

Table of Contents

———— ✺ ————

FOREWORD... xiii
PREFACE xv

Part One
Chapter 1. A Famine of Paternity upon the Earth 19
Chapter 2. Paternity vs. Paternalism................................. 22
Chapter 3. The Generations and Restoration 29
Chapter 4. The Honor of the Father 35
Chapter 5. Our Purpose 44

Part Two
Chapter 6. Three Parables that Illustrate Four Levels of
             Losses 52
Chapter 7. The Different Perspectives in the
             Father's House 59
Chapter 8. The Younger Son's Perspective 62
Chapter 9. The Older Son's Perspective............................ 67
Chapter 10. The Perspective of the Day Laborer
             ("Misthios") 73
Chapter 11. The Perspective of the Young Servant
             ("Pais") 80
Chapter 12. The Perspective of the Servant ("Doulos") 82
Chapter 13. Validation 87

Conclusion 90
Appendix.   Succession Planning... 101
Notes – Bibliography... 109
About the Author 111

Foreword

⎯⎯◦∞∞∞◦⎯⎯

Joshua Rodríguez is my friend. I have known Joshua, his wife, Paula, and his family for many years. I have ministered in his church on various occasions and I have a great respect for him as a pastor and leader in his community.

I have seen Joshua transform from a classical Pentecostal Christian into a man and leader with a new revelation from God. Joshua is a blessed man with higher education who could have lost years without seeing its fruit. He is free in theology and has a deep and refreshing message to share in *The Heart of the Father.*

Many of us in this world walk as spiritual orphans. Joshua invites us in this work to examine different levels of losses and how human beings respond to these. In Jeremiah 24:7 we read these words, "I will give them a heart to know me, that I am the LORD. They will be my people, and I will be their God, for they will return to me with all their heart."

This book deserves your time and I pray that you read it with a humble and open spirit.

-Nicky Cruz
Evangelist and Author

Preface

⸻⸦⸜⸝⸞⸟

We are living in a paternity crisis. Political, social, educational, and religious leaders document that the absence of effective parenting has produced a worldwide crisis in our generation. An undisputable sign of this crisis is the launching of *"The National Fatherhood Initiative"* in 2009 by President Barack Obama. Men and women without destiny and direction cry out for a healthy parenthood that reflects a commitment of love to its descendants. How many jails would be empty if we took on the mantle of a balanced paternity? How many frustrated leaders would breakthrough and flourish? We need hearts of true fathers and mothers to respond to this crisis. Finally, we have a faithful response to this lingering crisis.

In his book *The Heart of the Father*, Pastor Joshua Rodríguez gives us a book filled with refreshing and encouraging insight. This reflection is an exquisite offering for leaders, denominations, fathers, and mothers. I congratulate my great friend for saying "Enough already! We don't need any more paternalistic models that manipulate their offspring." In *The Heart of the Father*, we have a work established upon a healthy example of what it means to be restorative fathers and mothers. With the disappearance of reliable models, we had the proliferation of a paternalism that is deeply self-interested and castrating. The paternity that was projected in multiple pulpits and volumes at the end of the twentieth century was similar to the tragedy of *Oedipus the King* by Sophocles. In these reflections of *Oedipus the King,* we saw a tragic narcissistic paternity that fled from a commitment with the next generation.

Thanks to the contribution of Pastor Joshua, we do not have a tragedy based on conflicts between fathers and children, or institutions and their offspring, but instead we have a story that can restore and edify relationships. *The Heart of the Father* is not a tragedy, but a modern parable based on the narrative of the Restoring Father and the Prodigal Son. It is time that all of us (fathers, mothers, brothers and sisters) hear the challenge of our generation. Pastor Joshua directly presents the existential question of paternity: Will we chose to be devastating incubators, or cradles of divine purpose? As I read these pages, I heard myself saying, "Amen!" to the future generations cultivated with a restoring fraternity and paternity. Joshua, dear friend, thank you for truly loving and sowing. Long live fathers with love, and long live the younger brother!

Gabriel Salguero

President, National Latino Evangelical Coalition

Director, Institute for Faith and Public Life

Princeton Theological Seminary

PART

ONE

Chapter 1

A Famine of Paternity upon the Earth

The absence of paternity is not a new problem! In his era, the Apostle Paul had to fight with this challenge. He tells us in 1 Corinthians 4:14-15, "I am writing this not to shame you but to warn you as my dear children. Even if you had ten thousand guardians in Christ, you do not have many fathers, for in Christ Jesus I became your father through the gospel." The challenge of the famine of paternity is something quite old in human history.

Nowadays we have a problem that we must look at as an opportunity and it is the fact that there is a famine of paternity upon the Earth. In the first place, the United States has failed because since 1973, when the decision of *Roe vs. Wade,* was approved, it has aborted more than fifty-two million children. As fathers, we also have been responsible for the absence of a paternal figure.

The majority of homes in the United States are made up of children that do not live with both biological parents. As the Church, we have also contributed to the challenge of the lack of paternity in an enormous way. In our congregations, we have developed many teachers but few fathers. The word "guardians," which is translated from the word *paidagogos*, means "a tutor or guardian and guide to young people." Between the Greeks and the Romans, this name was applied to slaves worthy of trust; they were given to the responsibility and the charge of supervising the lives and morality of the children that belonged to the opulent class.

These young people were not allowed to leave the house until they reached an age of maturity. Paul affirms in 1 Corinthians 4:14 that there are many "guardians" within the people of God; in other words, there are many instructors and teachers, but there are few fathers that have the capacity and the heart to offer paternity. The effects of the lack of paternity in the lives of children are devastating. Allow me to share with you some of these effects:

- 50% of mothers do not see any value in the continued contact of fathers with their children. This means that many times the mothers cannot understand the damage and repercussion that the absence of paternity creates in children.[1]
- 90.2% of fathers with joint custody pay the financial support due.[2]
- 79.1% of fathers with visitation privileges pay the financial support due.[3]
- 44.5% of fathers with no visitation pay the financial support due.[4]
- 37.9% of fathers are denied any visitation.[5]
- 66% of all financial support not paid by non-custodial fathers is due to the inability to pay.[6]
- 63% of youth suicides are from fatherless homes.[7]
- 90% of all homeless and runaway children are from fatherless homes.[8]
- 85% of children that exhibit behavioral disorders come from fatherless homes.[9]
- 80% of rapists motivated by displaced anger come from fatherless homes.[10]
- 71% of all high school dropouts come from fatherless homes.[11]
- 70% of juveniles in state operated institutions come from fatherless homes.[12]
- 85% of all youth sitting in prisons grew up in a fatherless home.[13]

Nearly two of every five children in America do not live with their fathers.[14]

There are:

- 11,268,000 total custodial mothers[15]
- 2,907,000 total custodial fathers[16]

This means children in fatherless homes are:

- 4.6 times more likely to commit suicide[17]
- 6.6 times more likely to become teenage mothers (if they are girls, of course)[18]
- 24.3 times more likely to run away[19]
- 15.3 times more likely to have behavioral disorders[20]
- 6.3 times more likely to be in a state-operated institution[21]
- 10.8 times more likely to commit rape[22]
- 6.6 times more likely to drop out of school[23]
- 15.3 times more likely to end up in prison while a teenager[24]

Compared to children that are in the care of two biological, married parents—children who are in the care of single mothers are:

- 33 times more likely to be seriously abused (so that they will require medical attention) and[25]
- 73 times more likely to be killed.[26]

If we are to offer paternity in a biblical and effective manner, it is important to know the heart of our Heavenly Father and also the difference between paternity and paternalism.

Chapter 2

Paternity vs. Paternalism

One of the problems in our society is the distorted image of what the heart of the Heavenly Father is. Contributing to this image is the reality that many people confuse paternity with paternalism. Paternity is the state and quality of a father. A father is a man that has conceived a son. A father is also a person that exercises the function of guiding, directing, and instructing a child, so that the child is equipped with the necessary tools to have success in life and to fulfill his or her purpose in God.

On the other hand, paternalism is a protective attitude of a person that exercises authority. Paternity focuses on the leadership of the child and shows the child that God is the source of all guidance, while paternalism focuses the leadership on the life of the father and the father is presented as the source of all guidance. In paternity, children are equipped and trained to be able to hear the voice of God, while in paternalism the child is trained and equipped to learn how to hear the voice of the father in the house. An apostolic and prophetic ministry that is genuine and biblical operates under the principles of paternity not paternalism.

Paternity validates children, but paternalism only requires that children validate the father. In God's paternity, the inclusion and the power of each member of the body of Jesus Christ, (otherwise called the Church) is promoted. While in paternalism the exclusivity and the power of a clan or tribe is promoted. Some in the leadership field call this "specialism" which leads us to believe that we are better than everyone else.

I can speak to you from my own experience and tell you with all honesty that in the past I have been part of ecclesiastical groups that have presented their ideals and theological perspectives as the most accurate and precise within the body of Christ. We embraced this to the degree that we believed and erroneously taught that we were the most privileged in the Kingdom of God. Paternity in God shows us the contrary.

The Bible shows us that the Church is comprised of one body with many members and every member has a function. The Bible also teaches us in Romans 15:4, "For everything that was written in the past was written to teach us, so that through the endurance taught in the Scriptures and the encouragement they provide we might have hope." Therefore, we should learn from the examples of Israel as a nation, so that we are able to function under neotestamentary times. Israel had twelve tribes and each tribe had one specific function that differentiated it from the other tribes, but no tribe was more important than the other. Instead they collectively comprised what was the nation of Israel and in a very similar way, we form the body of Christ.

There are many tribes, denominations, ecclesiastical groups and even movements, but no group is better than any other, because we all enjoy the love, grace, favor and affection of our Father God. This is what the paternity of God teaches. However, paternalism teaches that privileged people exist including a remnant within a remnant in Christ, or rather that God has select and favorite children.

Paul says it in another way. He affirms that now in Christ Jesus, there is no Jew or Greek, no woman or man, and there is no free person or slave. Instead in Christ Jesus, we all enjoy the same privilege in regards to the love of God. God loves us all the same, and we all have access to the love, grace and favor of God the Father regardless of our different functions and assignments. I teach the brothers and sisters that I pastor, that regardless of how many blessings God pours over our lives and irrespective of how much grace and favor we experience as a local congregation, we should guard our hearts from competition, pride and arrogance within the body of Christ. We are not better than others, but instead enjoy an anointing and an impartation that God has given us as a local congregation.

Paternity teaches us that in the Kingdom of God there is no competition, instead we complement one another. By contrast, paternalism teaches us that we have to compete to be the best. In 1 Corinthians 1:12-13, the Apostle Paul brings correction to the brothers of Corinth and he tells them, "What I mean is this: One of you says, 'I follow Paul'; another, 'I follow Apollos'; another, 'I follow Cephas'; still another, 'I follow Christ.' Is Christ divided? Was Paul crucified for you? Were you baptized in the name of Paul?" Then in 1 Corinthians 3:6, Paul detains and confronts paternalism and says, "I planted the seed, Apollos watered it, but God has been making it grow." In other words, let us leave the competition, leave "specialism" and let us focus on the fact that all that we do, we do by the grace of God that has been poured over our lives.

Paternity seeks to teach children to create a dependency on God, while paternalism seeks to control the actions of children, creating a dependency on the father. Paternity seeks to serve children more than the children serve their father. In other words, servant leadership is modeled, while paternalism seeks to be served by children. Paternity encourages children to be original and not copies, while paternalism utilizes rules to control children in such a way that they become clones. In other words, paternalism uses the classical principle of mold structure, whereas paternity promotes that the unique characteristics in children excel and that the specific purpose of God be fulfilled in them.

Paternity seeks to develop maturity in children, while paternalism steals the process of maturity. In paternity, the father sacrifices so that his children can climb on his shoulders, while in paternalism the father climbs on the shoulders of his children. In paternity, fathers make the greatest investments of their life in their children, while in paternalism the fathers seek for children to make their greatest contributions and investments in the fathers.

In paternity, the diversity in thoughts and actions is promoted, while in paternalism unique thoughts and taking action is discouraged. In paternity, constructive criticism is received and the father is open to correction when brought forth respectfully, while paternalism does not allow the children to bring constructive criticism, much less bring loving correction.

In paternity, a powerful legacy is left for the children as well as the grandchildren, but in paternalism no beneficial legacy is left. Instead when the principle figure dies, the vision dies and is buried with him or her.

Paternity edifies others, while paternalism edifies self. In paternity, a clear vision and mission of the Kingdom exists, but with paternalism only a personal empire vision exists. In paternity, the father is willing to sacrifice his own life for his child, but in paternalism, the principal figure is ready to persecute and even kill his own children if his power is threatened.

God, the Father

God, as a Father, exercises paternity and not paternalism. We see this clearly in John 14 when Jesus says, "Don't you know me, Philip, even after I have been among you such a long time? Anyone who has seen me has seen the Father. How can you say, 'Show us the Father'? Don't you believe that I am in the Father, and that the Father is in me?" The mission of God as a Father is to show the world Jesus as Lord and Savior.

When we discuss paternity, it is important that the Father give a place to his child and understands that the child is in him, and he is in his child. For this reason, all of humanity knows Jesus as Savior of the world. One of the things that we need to do constantly is to hide so that our children grow and so that the world can see us through them. One of the greatest obstacles that prevent this development and this manifestation is insecurity. Regrettably, we have seen many models of leadership where insecurity leads fathers to break the children's "legs" and mistreat their kids, etc.

The Bible is filled with examples where God compares us to trees. One of the characteristics of this is when a new tree begins to grow. The trees that have been around longer in the forest can prevent the growth of smaller trees by overshadowing them to the point that if a smaller tree does not receive the light it needs to expand, its growth will be impeded and that tree will become stunted. Many times, insecurity will lead us to act in the same way when we see that a "small tree" has more potential, abilities, or gifts than us. Insecurity leads us to overshadow to the point that we make the growth life cycle of that small tree very difficult.

The Application

Another basic difference between paternity and paternalism is that in paternity, the mentor takes time to listen to the child and observe his or her development. They also invest time in the children to listen to them preach, see them minister, and help them to develop in a healthy manner. However, in paternalism, the mentor is so busy that he does not have time to listen to their children preach or teach, but he assumes a position of such importance that he never takes the time to sit down and listen to anyone else.

In paternity, a person understands that they can learn from even the smallest child who is the least prepared academically, while in paternalism, a person is blinded by arrogance and pride. Frequently, under this type of framework, a person is limited in the ability to learn from others.

Paternity embraces the principles of teaching like that of the Brazilian philosopher Paulo Freire. He sustained that the educational system, as a banking system, is not the most effective and does not allow all people to develop their potential. It is Freire's opinion, that the educational banking system occurs when the teacher acts as a bank and all of the students act as piggy banks that only exercise the function of receiving deposits of knowledge. Therefore, the students are not given the opportunity to deposit, share, or contribute to the growth and maturity of the teacher or their peers.

Giving the opportunity for all to contribute is known in the world of education as "teaching as a practice of freedom." In this method, the teacher does not just instruct his students, instead he lends himself to learn from them as well and thus continue his own journey of learning. In other words, in paternity a spirit of meekness exists, a docile spirit—where the mentor is willing to learn continually from his children. In this system, a person goes beyond the educational banking system, where the mentor projects the image that he has nothing to learn from his students or children.

In paternity, there is a respect and an appreciation for different styles of leadership or mentorship. In paternalism, there is much resistance to the styles of leadership that are different from one's own. Throughout the history of the church, we have seen the development and the manifestation of many different styles of leadership. It is very important to point out that despite your style of leadership, you should have a wise mentor that can share with you an external perspective of what you are doing. In this way, this person may provide a consistent balance to your leadership model.

Paternity or Genuine Mentorship

In paternity, genuine mentorship is experienced, while in paternalism, superficial mentorship is practiced. I would describe a genuine mentor as a person that combines Greco-Roman principles and methods with those of Hebrew roots, where not only is theory taught to the children, but the application in a real life environment is also given to them. That was Jesus' model. He did not just teach principles to his disciples and his children in the faith, but he also took them with him so they could learn practical things. According to some studies, 90% of what we learn, we learn visually, 9% we learn audibly and 1% we learn through other ways or methods.[1] In paternity, the principle of genuine mentorship is exercised utilizing Jesus' model:

- He did something as His spiritual children observed.
- He did something as His spiritual children assisted.
- He instructed them to do something as He helped them.
- They did something as He observed.
- They did something and would take someone with them so that disciple could observe.
- They did something and the disciple that was brought along assisted.
- The disciple did something as the person that had instructed him assisted.

- The new disciple did something and the person that instructed him observed.
- We note here that the cycle of discipleship or paternity is not complete until the spiritual child takes someone with them and imparts the same principles that were imparted to him through his mentor.

Chapter 3

The Generations and Restoration

There were 400 years of silence between the last book of the Old Testament (Malachi), and the first book of the New Testament Gospel narratives. However, the last thing the prophet Malachi declared before entering this period of silence is found in Malachi 4:4-6, "Remember the law of my servant Moses, the decrees and laws I gave him at Horeb for all Israel. See, I will send the prophet Elijah to you before that great and dreadful day of the LORD comes. He will turn the hearts of the fathers to their children, and the hearts of the children to their fathers; or else I will come and strike the land with total destruction."

If we are going to do everything that God has called us to do as a Church, it is important that we know our holy calling and the anointing God has poured over our lives. Malachi was prophesying about the restoration between fathers and their children. That is why he declared that God would turn the hearts of the fathers toward their children and the hearts of children toward their fathers.

It's interesting to note that in these verses Malachi is prophesying about the coming of the prophet Elijah. Elijah had already ascended to heaven without having known death in a whirlwind over 400 years before Malachi's prophecy. What then is the significance of this prophecy of restoration? First, more than 800 years after Elijah was lifted by a whirlwind into heaven, we find a prophetic word declared by the angel Gabriel before the birth of John the Baptist. The prophetic word in Luke 1:13-17 tells us,

> *But the angel said to him: "Do not be afraid, Zechariah; your prayer has been heard. Your wife Elizabeth will bear you a son, and you are to call him John. He will be a joy and delight to you, and many will rejoice because of his birth, for he will be great in the sight of the Lord. He is never to take wine or other fermented drink, and he will be filled with the Holy Spirit even before he is born. He will bring back many of the people of Israel to the Lord their God. And he will go on before the Lord, in the spirit and power of Elijah, to turn the hearts of the parents to their children and the disobedient to the wisdom of the righteous—to make ready a people prepared for the Lord."*

Jesus, speaking about John the Baptist, tells us in Matthew 11:10-14,

> *This is the one about whom it is written: "'I will send my messenger ahead of you, who will prepare your way before you." Truly I tell you, among those born of women there has not risen anyone greater than John the Baptist; yet whoever is least in the kingdom of heaven is greater than he. From the days of John the Baptist until now, the kingdom of heaven has been subjected to violence, and violent people have been raiding it. For all the Prophets and the Law prophesied until John. And if you are willing to accept it, he is the Elijah who was to come.*

This clearly indicates to us that John the Baptist came as a man with the spirit and the power of the prophet Elijah, with the purpose of turning the hearts of the fathers to their children, and the hearts of the children toward their fathers. John the Baptist also represented a typology of the church; therefore, to be able to understand a bit more about our calling as a church, we should study the life of John the Baptist and the life of the prophet Elijah.

The Prophet Elijah

Elijah was the father of prophets and was also a father to Elisha. That is why when Elijah said to Elisha, "Tell me, what I can do for you before I am taken from you?" Elisha replied, "Let me inherit a double portion of your spirit." Elisha was not asking for a natural or carnal birthright; he was asking for the blessing that a son expects from a father. He was not praying that God take his mentor. That is a false loyalty. That false loyalty was the spirit that manifested in the life of the youngest son in the parable of Luke 15, which we will discuss in another chapter.

When a child truly understands paternity, he does not want his father to die in any way. When we understand paternity, we truly value the relationship between a father and a child. When we apply paternity, only a chariot of fire can separate a father from their child. That is why when the *chariot of fire* separated Elisha from Elijah, Elisha began to cry out: *"My father! My father!"*

I certainly believe this was the invocation of ministerial orphanhood. In a sermon that I heard Pastor Juan Radhames Fernandez preach, he mentioned that the mantle that Elijah released symbolizes paternity, that is to say, the apostolic ministry. This sermon really shook me because I was able to receive a greater understanding of what paternity really means.

When we truly understand paternity, we seek the relationship with the father more than the mantle or the benefits that the father can give us. When a child looks for the father more than the mantle, the child is certainly worthy of that father's anointing. The mantle is not a position; instead it is all the father has in his spirit and transmits to his children.

The reason Elisha tore his clothing when Elijah ascended to heaven in a whirlwind is because he was in mourning over the parting of his spiritual father. That anointing of paternity, therefore, fell upon the life of the prophet Elisha.

The God of Generations

When God revealed himself to Moses, he did it as the God of Abraham, of Isaac, and of Jacob – that is to say, "The God of Generations." A generation is not limited to a time period of eighteen or forty years, because in Genesis 15:16, God said to Abraham: "In the fourth generation your descendants will come back here, for the sin of the Amorites has not yet reached its full measure." In other words in the fourth generation, his children would return and his descendants would come back to worship and live in the land of Canaan.

When we study generations, we learn that a generation is not simply something we look at in terms of time, but in terms of massive movements of people. If a generation was only about forty years, then the word God gave Abraham in Genesis15 would have been fulfilled in no more than 160 years. When we study the Bible carefully and gain clarity, we learn that this prophetic word took more than 400 years to be fulfilled; thus a biblical generation is defined as a massive movement of people.

The first generation (the first massive movement) was guided by Abraham when he moved from Mesopotamia to Canaan. The second generation took place under the leadership of Jacob, when he moved with seventy men from Canaan to Egypt. The third generation occurred under the leadership of Moses, when God called him and used him to be the liberator of the people of Israel, and he took them out of Egypt and brought them into the desert. The fourth generation was led by Joshua, when he directed the people of Israel from the desert into Canaan. In this fourth generation, or massive movement of people, the prophetic word that God had spoken to Abraham in Genesis 15:16 was fulfilled.

The Modern Generations

At this time, God is raising a movement of people that are willing to listen to his voice with clarity and willing to work diligently to positively impact every segment of our society. When we historically study the generations of our nation, we find that God rose up a strong and hardworking generation in the early 1900's that resembled Abraham and his peers. According to sociologists, this generation is known as the Builder Generation. This group was born before 1945 and was responsible for winning World War II. They were so hard working that when returning from the war in 1945, they began to give birth to millions of babies born between 1946 and 1964.

In an eighteen year period, approximately thirty to thirty-five million children were born, but when the Builder Generation returned from World War II, there was a supernatural multiplication of births. For that reason, the children that were born during this period are known as the "Baby Boomers." In that historic period of eighteen years more than seventy million babies were born.

From 1965 to 1983 another generation was born known as Generation X. This generation was given this name because they had many challenges, especially with their identity. Generation Y (Why?), which was born between the years 1984 and 2002. This is a generation that lacks paternity and it is also known as the *Bridgers* Generation. They are sometimes referred to as *Bridgers* because they serve as a link between two centuries and two millenniums.

Every generation has strengths and weaknesses. Every generation makes choices and decisions that will affect other generations to come. In 1973, the Supreme Court of the United States of America approved *Roe vs. Wade*, and as a result of this law that legalized abortion, we have been responsible for the deaths of more than fifty-two million children. These were leaders whose potential was never fulfilled. Tragically, when we look at all the problems that this generation (also known as Bridgers) will have to face, we are amazed. All of their challenges and problems are things their fathers should have confronted for them. It is also a generation that lacks paternity because many of these children or young people live in a home where both biological parents are not present.

Many experts agree that the Bridgers Generation or Generation "Why?" have several challenges before them. First, they face economic uncertainty. Secondly, they face a lack of moral boundaries and thirdly, they live in a society where the culture has a daily increase in violence. Fourthly, they are faced with a lack of clarity in their roles as men and women. Lastly, they face the most serious problem of all–**a severe crisis of faith**. They are being raised in a world without values and without principles, and while they take an interest in spiritual things, they have practically no interest in what society calls "organized religion."

I believe that this is a magnificent opportunity for the Church of Jesus Christ to stand up and walk with the anointing of Elijah and John the Baptist, returning the hearts of the fathers toward their children and the hearts of the children toward their fathers.

The question is then: *What can the church do with this opportunity?* Let's start by modeling economic stability and showing this new generation that they must abandon the consumer mindset and apply the biblical mindset of being investors. We can show them that bad is bad and good is good, and that the Word of God teaches us with clarity the principles and values that honor and please the heart of God as a Father. We also need to validate the identity of our children. As fathers, today more than ever before, we have to show our children what it means to be men and women of God, by adequately providing spiritual leadership before them in the style of the true servant.

Chapter 4

The Honor of the Father

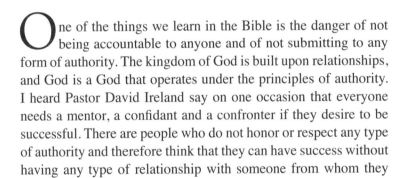

One of the things we learn in the Bible is the danger of not being accountable to anyone and of not submitting to any form of authority. The kingdom of God is built upon relationships, and God is a God that operates under the principles of authority. I heard Pastor David Ireland say on one occasion that everyone needs a mentor, a confidant and a confronter if they desire to be successful. There are people who do not honor or respect any type of authority and therefore think that they can have success without having any type of relationship with someone from whom they can learn. The principle of honor is fundamental in understanding the heart of God as a paternal figure.

In Gene Edwards's book titled, "*A Tale of Three Kings*," he presents three types of paternal perspectives in leadership. He presents King Saul as the leader that is selected by men, and later confirmed by God for a society with hardened hearts. Saul represents the leader that walks well for a time period, but later strays because of perversity, obstinacy, and rebellion in his heart.

Edwards also presents Absalom as the second model for paternal leadership. He represents someone who places and calls himself to exercise a function that God never called him to exercise. Edwards also presents the leadership model of David to exemplify someone who is separated, called, and sent by God. David represents the leader who governs according to the heart of God.

David was not perfect, but he knew how to humble himself and bow his heart before God when he made mistakes. David also learned to model what is subjection and submission to authority, even when authority derailed from God's purposes. David was loyal to Saul until the last day of his life. Even though Saul persecuted him and wanted to kill him, David resisted all temptation to attempt to take Saul's life. In 1 Samuel 24:5, we find something very interesting and it says: "Afterward, David was conscience-stricken for having cut off a corner of his robe."

David had the opportunity to kill Saul for persecuting him unjustly. Instead he opted to forgive his life and to simply cut the edge of his robe off. The Bible says that the heart of David was conscience-stricken for only having cut the edge of Saul's robe. When we read this in English it doesn't appear to be a big deal, but when we read it in Hebrew, we can better comprehend the gravity of what David did. It is then that we are able to better understand the reason why David's heart trembled.

God rejected Saul and told Samuel the prophet to stop advocating on his behalf. Yet Samuel persisted to intercede for him and asked God to have mercy. In spite of this, David remained loyal and submitted to the authority of Saul. David did not attempt to take the throne because he understood that God was responsible for placing kings and removing kings. Please bear in mind that Samuel himself anointed and separated David as the next king of Israel, and Jonathan, his best friend had taken off his royal robe and had placed it upon him. In spite of this, David still waited patiently for the day when God would remove Saul. He refused to do this on his own.

David trembled before God because what he cut from the edge of the kingly robe is what Hebrew teaches us was the "*kanaph*." The "*kanaph*" was the "border" of the robe. This Hebrew word is utilized to describe the border or the edge of a person's robe and it is also the same word that is utilized to describe the "wings" of a dove or a bird. The kings and people of opulence in those days displayed their rank and power on their "*kanaph*," that is to say the border of their robe. Many of the kings had the custom of having gold, silver, and precious stones on the edge of their robe, in such a way that when a person looked at the rim of the robe they were able to see the rank and the weight of the authority that person had.

When David cut Saul's "*kanaph,*" he did not just cut a piece of fabric from his robe. No, no, no no...he prophetically cut his rank, his authority, and that was why his heart trembled. His heart trembled because although what he had done was simply a prophetic act, he had much respect and fear for those that God placed in authority. The Hebrew word for "conscience-stricken" in 1 Samuel 24:5 is the word "*nakah.*" The word "*nakah*" means, "*to crush, conquer, and bring judgment upon.*" What David felt was that his heart judged him for cutting the symbolic rank of his king, Saul.

Confronting a Father

I did not grasp this principle until I made the grave mistake of rebelling against authority during my younger years. During that time I was leading the youth ministry of the ecclesiastical organization that I was a part of. I erroneously thought that when I had a difference of opinion with my leader, that is to say my lead pastor, I had the right to confront him publicly and to debate him in front of 200 people in order to present my perspective and my ideas.

I caused much harm and pain to my spiritual father due to my immaturity and ignorance. I simply had the wrong perspective of the heart of the Father. As a result of this serious error that I committed, the leadership of the ecclesiastical organization that I was working with decided to take severe action towards me. Today, I give God thanks for the correction they brought to my life. At that time, I was very naïve and did not understand. I give God thanks for the body of leaders who dealt with me strongly and with little mercy because I really needed to go through that process to understand and value what I understand and value today – the heart of the Father.

In a moment of confrontation certain privileges and functions I was exercising at the denominational leadership level were taken from me. Some who did not understand God's dealings with me at that time, supported me and said, "We are going to protest through public manifestations and via media communications because of what they have done to you and if they don't retract, we will go to court." I decided to go into a spiritual retreat and seek the heart of God. In those days, I shut myself in, and I was able to hear the voice of God speak to my heart. It was not an audible voice, instead it was a voice that spoke to my conscience and my heart and it said: "Son, be silent and humble yourself because I am going to show you my justice. I am going to show you what you have to go through because of my justice."

I had not understood that in the Cross of Calvary, through the redeeming work of Jesus, there was a symbolic union between mercy and the justice of God. I did not understand that in the cross we find perfect balance of what mercy and justice is, but through my personal experience, God was showing me a great lesson regarding appreciation for God's authority. During this personal time that I was able to have with God, I was ministered to by the Holy Spirit and by the Word of God in regard to the importance of submitting to authority even when I thought that I had been a victim of spiritual abuse.

God wanted to show me that no one cares more about his Church than Him, and He does not need a lawyer and much less a judge, because His is the power forever and ever. The question is then, does a child have the right to confront a father? I believe that moments exist when the circumstances and opportunity present themselves to have a dialogue of correction with a paternal figure. There is a correct and respectful manner for a child to confront a father, or for a person to confront a mentor, or a person to whom they are accountable.

I believe that as fathers we should open ourselves up to correction so that those people we serve can come to us with any concern they have in regard to us. It is one thing to cover the nakedness of the father, and another to ignore it. Covering is not ignoring. Genesis 9:20-24 says:

> *The sons of Noah who came out of the ark were*
> *Shem, Ham and Japheth. (Ham was the father of*
> *Canaan.) These were the three sons of Noah, and*
> *from them came the people who were scattered*
> *over the whole earth. Noah, a man of the soil, pro-*
> *ceeded to plant a vineyard. When he drank some*

of its wine, he became drunk and lay uncovered inside his tent. Ham, the father of Canaan, saw his father naked and told his two brothers outside. But Shem and Japheth took a garment and laid it across their shoulders; then they walked in backward and covered their father's naked body. Their faces were turned the other way so that they would not see their father naked. When Noah awoke from his wine and found out what his youngest son had done to him, he said, "Cursed be Canaan! The lowest of slaves will he be to his brothers."

The problem with Ham was that when he saw the nakedness of his father Noah, he did not cover him. Shem and Japheth heard about the nakedness thanks to Ham, but refused to see their father's nakedness. They put garments across their shoulders and walked backwards, covering the nakedness of their father. Covering is not hiding sin; instead, it is guiding those that have fallen in such a way that they can be restored. Covering is doing exactly what the father did with his son in the parable of the prodigal son. He found him, confronted him, rescued him, saved him, healed him, forgave him, and restored him.

Moments exist in ministry when the confrontations need to be stronger. We find the classic example of this in Galatians when Paul confronts the Apostle Peter. In Galatians 2: 11-14, it says:

When Cephas came to Antioch, I opposed him to his face, because he stood condemned. For before certain men came from James, he used to eat with the Gentiles. But when they arrived, he began to draw back and separate himself from the Gentiles because he was afraid of those who belonged to the circumcision group. The other Jews joined him in his hypocrisy, so that by their hypocrisy even Barnabas was led astray. When I saw that they were not acting in line with the truth of the gospel, I said to Cephas in front of them all, "You are a Jew, yet you live like a Gentile and not like

*a Jew. How is it, then, that you force Gentiles to
follow Jewish customs?"*

When Peter came to Antioch, Paul had to oppose him to his
face, because he stood condemned. Here we learn that there is
a correct way to confront people who are in authority over our
lives. Observe well that the Apostle Paul confronted Peter in front
of leadership, and he also wrote a letter to all the brothers in the
region of Galatia to the point that more than 1800 years later, you
and I are learning about this confrontation. Paul not only confronted Peter, but he wanted the whole world to know that his
mentor, Barnabas, also became involved in compromising the
message of grace of the Kingdom of God, and verse 13 says that
Barnabas was also led astray due to their hypocrisy.

On another occasion, Paul had a very strong and respectful
confrontation with his mentor Barnabas, the person who had discipled him for many years. They had a conflict concerning the
theme of paternity, because Paul's ministerial philosophy was different than that of Barnabas regarding the restoration of a young
man named John Mark. Their ministerial conflict caused a sep-
aration, and although Barnabas appealed to **mercy** and Paul to
justice, after many years Paul changed his perspective and sent
for John Mark. After a time of processing, Paul thought that Mark
was now useful for the ministry.

Therefore, I believe there is a precise moment and a proper
manner to confront fathers. It should always be done with love,
respect and the correct spirit because fathers can learn a lot from
their children and children from their fathers. For this reason,
fathers need to take more time to share and to listen to their children, and in this way observe them and their level of development.

I believe that it is very dangerous when a person develops
so much that he can no longer sit to listen to his children speak,
because he has lost his spirit of meekness that enables him to continue learning. It is dangerous to hear people say, "I already know
what this person is going to speak or preach about; I already know
what he is going to say." These declarations steal from us the
experience of continuous learning.

A Second Father

In 1989, as a young single man, I fell in love with a beautiful young lady named Paula. A year and a half later we got married, and as I entered her family, I fell in love with them too. Her parents adopted me as a son in their home and I enjoyed the privilege, of having a second father and not just a father-in-law. My father-in-law was not perfect – he had many weaknesses and many imperfections –and although he was not a Christian man, he was a man who loved his family and emphasized harmony and closeness between children and parents.

Sometimes I would ask myself how it was possible for a family to have so much love for a man that committed so many mistakes and had so many weaknesses. The truth is that this man allowed himself to be loved and provoked in others the desire to love him. I was his son, I was his friend, and on many occasions I was his counselor and his confronter. Through the years we were able to see the seed of the Word of God growing in him and how in times of trials and tribulations, he knew where to go.

He had learned something of great value. He learned that in the midst of difficulties and of human rebellion caused by sin, the throne of God was a throne of grace, favor, mercy and forgiveness for all those who drew near with repentant hearts.

On May 9, 2007, I decided to plan a romantic night with my wife Paula, taking her out to dinner and having her participate with me in a twenty-four hour celebration in the city of Paris, France. We arrived in Paris on a Thursday morning and the next day, early in the afternoon, we were on our way back to our home. It was a day that we will never forget in our entire lives. In only one day we were able to enjoy a marvelous time where we delighted in a candlelight dinner on a yacht over the river *Le Seine*. It was one of the most romantic moments that we have had in our twenty plus years of marriage. In just one day, I believe we grew ten years in our marriage because it was something unforgettable. I believe that investing in your marriage is one of the best investments that one can make in life. Just as the MasterCard commercial says, "It is ***priceless***."

It all played out like a movie, but as we returned home that Friday afternoon, we received the bad news that a young man we grew up with had passed on to eternity due to a sudden illness. Although we were exhausted due to the trip, we went to New York to be with the family and offer our condolences. The last thought in our minds was that our night of mourning was just beginning.

When we returned home late that night after being at the funeral home, we were still feeling the effects of the trip and the jet lag. We went to bed and in less than an hour, the phone rang. It was about 12:15 in the morning when my wife picked up the phone and I could hear the screams from my mother-in-law that said, "He is dying, he is dying, your dad is dying!" Paula called 911 and immediately ran to my in-law's house, since they lived close to us.

She was able to arrive at the same time as the paramedics. My father-in-law had suffered a heart attack and when Paula arrived, she was able to witness the last breath her father experienced. When I received the news, my heart was paralyzed, because in less than two years I had now lost both of my fathers. All the inspiration I had received from the last twenty-four hours in Paris with my wife was something that God allowed to bring us from one extreme of happiness to then another extreme of mourning and sadness. Now again my spirit and my soul cried out, "My father, my father."

The only thing that consoled me was knowing that as my father-in-law experienced the heart attack and said to my mother-in-law, "I am dying, I am dying," she instructed him, "Cry out to God. Get your life right with God." In that moment, all of the Word of God that was in him was able to be manifested and he was able to ask God for forgiveness and settle his accounts with God. He was also able to cry out to God as a father and say, "My father, my father, forgive me for my sins and save me."

It is so good to know that even the transgressions and mistakes one has committed in life do not prevent the fulfillment of the word declared by the psalmist in Psalms 51:17 which says, "My sacrifice, O God, is a broken spirit; a broken and contrite heart you, God, will not despise."

When a person repents and draws near to God with a contrite and humble heart, that person will enjoy all of God the Father's favor, grace, mercy and forgiveness. When there is genuine repentance, the scene of the returning prodigal son displayed in Luke chapter 15 plays out: the Father is moved to mercy, runs towards the child, throws his arms around him and kisses him.

Chapter 5

Our Purpose

I t is our faith in God as Father, and the validation of our children that helps us to answer the question, "*Why are we on this earth?*" A person will never find their purpose in life, which will take him toward God's destiny, without first knowing his origin or identity. Some time ago, we began to do a little research about our true identity and origin. We began to study a little anatomy, biology and physiology and we discovered an element of faith in these sciences. We discovered that there is a champion hidden inside every human being that is walking upon this planet. When is it that we begin life? Some people say at twelve weeks of a woman's pregnancy, other say at twenty weeks. Others say that it is at the moment of conception; others use the argument of the prophet Jeremiah who said that life begins when we are in our mother's womb, etc. What we do know is that life begins as a race. We do not know if it was in the early morning, in the afternoon, or at night, but it all began when our biological parents shared a moment of intimacy. When they had that encounter, out of your father came a river that included anywhere between 200 million to 500 million swimmers.

It is interesting that science teaches us that this swimming race began *against the current* and that only a few were going to make it to the *finals*. There are adults and even young people who say that they do not know how to swim, when the truth is that they forgot, because if they had not known how to swim, they would have never made it where they are today.

Some time ago you were in a race that began in a river, and you were swimming against the current. Only the most aggressive and most determined swimmer was going to win the race. This race had one final competition that took place in the "Fallopian tubes." You were there waiting for the commencement of the final competition. You were simply waiting for one little egg to appear and somehow there was something inside of you that was leading you to persevere and to not give up, even though you had no eyesight, because your little eyes had not been formed yet.

Someone was helping you along the way and I believe with all of my heart it was the Holy Spirit. All this time you were swimming against the current, because from the beginning of life, God had designed you to navigate against the current. When you know your identity, you will not allow any lie to govern your life. It is assumed that when the world tells you that something cannot be done, you lift your voice and say, "Yes it can, because I have been designed by God to go against the current."

The Head, Not the Tail

When our government lacks solutions or answers to many of the social problems that we face today as a nation, you and I as part of the body of Jesus Christ, have to say, "Yes, there is a solution and we have it." Problems exist, but in Christ Jesus those problems become opportunities for those whose hope transcends the most difficult challenges that the world can present. You are more than a conqueror; you are a champion. The evidence of this lies in that you reached the finish line. Only a few remained in the last round. The first swimmer that introduced his little head through the exterior layer of the egg would be declared the winner. When you introduced your head inside the little egg, there was a chemical reaction, the outer wall of the egg was sealed, and as a result, your tail was cut off. The reason why your tail was cut off is because all of the genetic coding that you needed in order to develop was in your head. The tail only served as a device to move you. While I studied this, the Holy Spirit brought to memory

Deuteronomy 28:13 which says, "The Lord will make you the head, not the tail. If you pay attention to the commands of the Lord your God that I give you this day and carefully follow them, you will always be at the top, never at the bottom."

This is when I understood that we have truly been designed to be the head and not the tail. When you understand your identity, you live how God designed you to live. When you understand your identity, you can look at the *tail* as simply an instrument designed by God to take you to a destination or a determined place. Why is it then that so many people live like *tails*, even though they were designed by God to live like a head? The answer is simple: they do not comprehend their identity and therefore, even if the purpose of the tail was to be a means of transportation to take them to a determined place, they continue to live like a tail instead of living like a head. That is why the Bible teaches us that we are designed by God to be always on top and not on the bottom. I was at a leaders conference in Guadalajara Mexico some time ago and I shared this identity principle. After I was done speaking two people in the audience who identified themselves as medical doctors approached me. They asked me: "Did you know that when the little sperm enters the egg there is a type of formation at the top of his or her head that bears the appearance of a crown?" I responded and simply said, "wow." This was amazing to hear. As part of our identity God has supernaturally crowned us with favor even before we were born.

Did you also know that you won this race without eyes? That is why the Bible says that you and I have been designed by God to walk by faith and not by sight. "For we live by **faith**, not by **sight**" (2 Corinthians 5:7). From the beginning of your life, God had already deposited faith and vision inside your spirit and your training process did not end there. Later, God himself formed you inside your mother's womb, and for nine months gave you the ability to grow, to develop and to be nourished in the midst of a dark, uncomfortable and limited space.

Joey Palmerini

This particular message of faith and of hope was what captivated the attention of one of our sons in the faith. This was the message that allowed Joey Palmerini, a twelve-year-old boy with physical and emotional impediments, to come to our congregation when the state of New Jersey had failed in providing him a safe and healthy environment where he could develop and grow. Our son Joey was involved in a horrible car accident that left him with serious physical disabilities. This occurred at the age of seven, and because of this accident he had to have a tracheotomy. He suffered permanent damages to his body; he limped and also suffered greatly in his emotional development. Joey was twelve years old when God gave us the privilege to meet him. Where were his mother and his father? His biological father was in jail for mistreating and abusing him. His mother and his stepfather suffered from drug abuse. Joey was a kid that knew the streets and walked them with shrewdness and in an impressive manner. He knew how to make money by panhandling.

When we met Joey, he did not like to bathe and as a result, at times it was very difficult to be around him for long periods of time. When Joey turned sixteen, his mother and stepfather had already passed away. Joey was now alone, but one day, by the favor and the grace of God, Joey heard and received a message of faith that resulted in a miracle. As a result of this miraculous conversion, Joey Palmerini became one of the ministers of our congregation at Cityline Church.

Joey was like one of my own biological sons. He learned personal hygiene, respect, loyalty, and above all things, that he was special and **a true champion.** His transformation sometimes left us shocked, how a young man that hated to bathe was now bathing twice a day.

One day I felt the need in my heart to celebrate his next birthday in a great way. I called together the entire congregation, and I invited them to celebrate his birthday in an unforgettable manner. Everyone was moved and together we organized a party that shook him. It was such a surprise that when Joey entered the birthday location, he was stunned. Later we learned that no one had ever celebrated his birthday to that magnitude in his entire life. Joey received so many gifts that day that he did not know how to respond to so much love, and above all to the power of affirmation and validation. For us it was the most memorable and most significant birthday celebration we have ever participated in.

Unfortunately, after this historic celebration and miraculous transformation, Joey was diagnosed with cancer at the age of twenty. All of a sudden, people visited us from many state agencies that somehow, throughout all these years, were responsible for Joey's life. Joseph Palmerini had been another victim, lost inside of a failed social service system.

We experienced four painful months together with him during intensive chemotherapy. After the chemotherapy, the prognosis was very good, but Joey did not take care of himself and in the middle of winter he always walked around without buttoning his coat. As a result, Joey caught a cold that later turned into a respiratory infection. In less than ninety days after having completed his chemotherapy, Joey died.

The day that Joey died, I was able to experience something in my heart that I had never felt. It is so difficult to explain with words, because it is a profound and physical feeling. It was as if a part of my body died. When I received the phone call from the hospital that he only had hours to live, I cried at home as if this spiritual son had come out from my own loins. As a father, it was a very difficult moment for me. It was a moment that marked my life forever.

I was able to understand a little better the scene in *Golgotha* when Jesus handed over his Spirit and God the father saw him die. I was in the hospital room when Joey took his last breath. I was able to understand and feel the paternal pain that comes when a child dies ahead of a parent. It is supposed to be that the children bury their parents and not that the parents have the great responsibility and burden to bury their children, but sometimes the unexplainable occurs.

I believed God was going to heal him, that He was going to lift him up, and that He was going to do greater things with him. Joey's conversion was so radical and so impressive that, as a father, I was able to picture him married with children. I could already see him maturing to a level higher than society had determined for him. I had the faith that God was going to heal him and raise him, but it wasn't so. God had other plans that were not mine. His life was not a failure, because God destined him to be more than a conqueror.

Words of Affirmation

One of the powerful weapons God has given us as fathers to propel our children to grow is the declaration of words that mark them positively. I am referring to positive words that bless them and that catapult them toward God's purpose and destiny for their lives. The absence of healthy words can limit the growth of a person.

I will never forget the experience I had in the fifth grade at the age of ten, when a teacher negatively marked me with words. This teacher did not know how to motivate me to be a better student, and she used negative words to attempt to motivate all the students in the class. It was the only time in my life that I had failed a course and this truly worked negatively in my mind.

The next scholastic year when I entered the sixth grade, I met a teacher that I will never forget. She was used by God to change my life forever. This teacher was a young Jewish woman named Sherry Perlowitz. From the moment she began to teach me in the sixth grade, she saw in me a purpose and a destiny. She began to use positive words to guide me towards a better and healthier academic life.

This teacher began to mark my destiny with words and phrases like: "You are brilliant!" "You can be an outstanding student." "You can walk with more firmness." "You can run at a faster speed" and "You can fly much higher than what you are flying." These words led me to see immediate results in my academic progress.

In a few months, this woman of God had motivated me in such a way that my level of reading increased to a level higher than that of a ninth grader and my math level had reached higher than an eighth grade level. This happens when we use words that affirm and edify people. This woman's words affirmed me, and this is why it is important that we also affirm our biological children and our spiritual children and declare over them powerful achievements that they are to reach by the grace of God.

PART

TWO

Chapter 6

Three Parables that Illustrate Four Levels of Losses

In Luke 15, we find a powerful and radical teaching of Jesus concerning three parables. A parable is a short story that illustrates a moral, spiritual or heavenly lesson. The language of the East abounds with figurative language. "Parable" comes from the Greek word *parabol* and it signifies to put one thing next to the other.

A parable places the natural and the spiritual things side by side with the goal of presenting a spiritual teaching. A parable illustrates truths that require eyes, ears, and hearts with the grace to see, to listen, and understand the mysteries of the Kingdom of God. For this reason, Jesus explains in Matthew 13:18-23,

> *Listen then to what the parable of the sower means: When anyone hears the message about the kingdom and does not understand it, the evil one comes and snatches away what was sown in their heart. This is the seed sown along the path. The seed falling on rocky ground refers to someone who hears the word and at once receives it with joy. But since they have no root, they last only a short time. When trouble or persecution comes because of the word, they quickly fall away. The seed falling among the thorns refers to*

> *someone who hears the word, but the worries of*
> *this life and the deceitfulness of wealth choke the*
> *word, making it unfruitful. But the seed falling on*
> *good soil refers to someone who hears the word*
> *and understands it. This is the one who produces*
> *a crop, yielding a hundred, sixty or thirty times*
> *what was sown.*

We need to listen, understand and produce fruit as a result of the impartation that we receive through a parable. May you allow God to give you eyes, ears and a heart with the grace to see, listen and understand the mysteries of the Kingdom of God enclosed in the three parables of Luke 15. My prayer is that you are able to hear God in such a way that you are willing to change because of what you hear.

The translators of the Bible throughout the years have titled these parables, "The Parable of the Lost Sheep," "The Parable of the Lost Coin," and "The Parable of the Prodigal Son." In these three parables, Jesus makes use of a well-known literary tool called hyperbole. Hyperbole is a literary resource that is utilized with the goal of stirring the feelings or the emotions of people. When we look at what the word *hyperbole* means, we find that some define it as an exaggeration. But an exaggeration has many contexts. An exaggeration is a much bigger representation of reality. Exaggeration is also defined in this way: *to enlarge or increase especially beyond the normal proportions.* In the context of using hyperbole as a literary tool to stir the senses, Jesus applies it with the goal of magnifying and expanding the degree of God's love for humanity.

In other words, when we examine chapter 15 of the book of Luke closely, we learn that the love of God as a Father is an exaggeration. It goes far beyond what the normal proportion of human love is. Therefore, the intention of the parable of the lost sheep, of the lost coin, and of the prodigal son is to present the love, the grace, and the favor of God as a father.

When we study each parable in Luke 15, we observe or learn that Jesus utilizes hyperbole as a tool to move the feelings of the audience. Excellent communicators study their audiences before speaking to them. The first thing we learn in verse one is that Jesus came near to talk to the tax collectors and sinners. Each parable – of the lost sheep, of the lost coin, and of the prodigal son – is about financial resources because the tax collectors were people in their society that were lovers of money.

It is for this reason that Jesus uses hyperbole to demonstrate the intensity of the losses in each parable. In the first parable, the loss is only of one percent. Only one percent of the sheep in the fold get lost. In the second parable, the loss is of ten percent. Only one coin of ten was lost. But in the third parable, the father experiences a loss of fifty percent because one of two children is lost. In the end, the son experiences a 100 percent loss because he completely moved away from his Father. A child has only one father, and to lose his father indicates that he has lost it all.

These three parables suggest that God suffers for the loss of each person that moves away from him. These three parables also manifest that when God feels compassion for the loss of human beings, He is moved to take action. These parables also express what the love of God means for us and show us the abundant joy that God experiences as a result of the restoration of the sinner. The first two parables illustrate the intervention of God, and how it is that Jesus was moved to look for what he had lost. That is to say, Jesus Christ goes out to look for the sinner with the goal of saving him, healing him, and restoring his relationship with the Father.

The third parable clearly illustrates how it is that human beings respond to the Father and how it is that the sinner or the lost man returns to the Father's house. When we combine the three parables, we can see God searching for man and man searching for God.

The Parable of the Lost Sheep

In the first parable, nestled within the story is a question. "Suppose one of you has a hundred sheep and loses one of them. Doesn't he leave the ninety-nine in the open country and go after the lost sheep until he finds it?" (Luke 15:3-4) When we look at this question through a Western lens, we don't understand the reply. To understand the correct reply for this question, we have to put on the cultural lenses of the people that live in the East. One of the things we learned in seminary with our Hebrew professor, Dr. Bryan Widbin, is that in this teaching the question is a ridiculous question, and the answer is, "No one!" Why? Because it was not economically feasible. It was not worth the risk to leave ninety-nine sheep behind to go on an adventure after one, but Jesus Christ was stirring the feelings of his audience and was expanding their way of thinking.

When we study the parable thoroughly, we see that Jesus is trying to establish a Kingdom principle for them. Although no common shepherd in his time was willing to leave behind ninety-nine sheep with the goal of saving one lost sheep, there was a shepherd known by Jesus who was willing to go against the current and do something uncommon. He was willing to leave the flock behind and take all the necessary risks with the goal of finding, saving and restoring one sheep that had been lost.

What Jesus was trying to teach them was a lesson of love. He wanted them to understand that when someone loves a sheep in such an extraordinary way, that sheep is worth the same as the other sheep collectively. Jesus was establishing the principle of the love of God for humanity. There is no price that can be placed on the restoration of a lost soul in the eyes of God. Those listening in the audience were scratching their heads and thinking, "In what world does he live in?" No shepherd that has 100 sheep and loses one is going to take the risk of leaving to go after it, instead he will count it as lost. For the audience and especially for the tax collectors that examined and analyzed everything under a financial magnifying glass, this was something ridiculous, incongruous and without common rationalization.

Jesus was trying to teach them about the joy of restoration. While none of them were willing to risk everything for one small lost sheep, he knew a person, a shepherd that would go way beyond what was considered normal or common. This shepherd would not just look for the sheep, but he'd find the sheep, joyfully carry it home on his shoulders, and heal it. He would then gather his friends and neighbors and invite them to a celebration because he had found his lost sheep. Jesus gave them the meaning behind the parable and said: "I tell you that in the same way there will be more rejoicing in heaven over one sinner who repents than over ninety-nine righteous persons who do not need to repent" (Luke 15:7). In other words, any sinner that needs salvation causes joy, and even more joy in heaven when he repents, than ninety-nine people considered righteous that do not need to repent. God loves the sinner in such a way that He is willing to take the greatest risk with the goal of finding, redeeming, saving and restoring him.

The Parable of Lost Coin

Surely in that moment, many of the tax collectors in the audience were thinking that this was not economic wisdom. The Lord continued in verse 8 by asking: "Or suppose a woman has ten silver coins and loses one. Doesn't she light a lamp, sweep the house and search carefully until she finds it?" If you and I try to answer this question with Western lenses, again we fail. The answer is, "No." No woman who has ten silver coins and loses one is going to take her time to turn on the lamp, sweep her house and look diligently for one coin because economically it is not practical to do. But here again, Jesus is utilizing hyperbole as a tool to stir the feelings of his audience, especially the tax collectors who were such lovers of money.

In this parable then, Jesus explained that this woman did something out of the ordinary such as light a lamp, sweep the entire house and search with diligence until she found this lost silver coin. He said that when the woman found her lost coin, she gathered her friends and neighbors saying, "Rejoice with me because I have found the silver coin that I had lost" (Luke 15:9). That is when Jesus again gave them the meaning or the revelation of the parable.

He doesn't stop there but brings the message home by telling them, "In the same way, I tell you, there is rejoicing in the presence of the angels of God over one sinner who repents" (Luke 15:10). In other words, what does not make sense economically for the tax collectors is of much value for God. The Lord Jesus was breaking their paradigm.

He was shaking that mindset and was trying to establish that the love of God for the lost is so great that it has no price. The price that God is willing to pay for the salvation and restoration of one sinner is enormous, and confuses the common mindset. At this point in the conversation, the audience could not comprehend what Jesus was communicating to them. He was truly shaking the people's paradigm. I am sure that they were scratching their heads and saying, "This makes no sense."

The Parable of the Prodigal Son

We need to understand that the first parable established the principle of love and grace. The second parable reaffirmed it and the third parable cemented the principle. The third parable is what many writers have titled "The Parable of the Lost Son." I want to submit for your consideration that the title "The Parable of the Prodigal/Lost Son" is not the best title for the story that is expressed in Luke 15:11-32.

One of the first things we need to do when we study a scriptural passage of the Bible is to look for the central theme of the verses we are examining. When we read the content of this parable carefully, we can conclude that the central theme is not, "the lost son." The central theme is all about "the love, the favor, and the grace of the father."

Therefore we would have to ask ourselves one question, and that question would be: What motived the translators of the Bible to give this parable the title of, "The Parable of the Lost or Prodigal Son?" The answer has to do with the fact that the father in the parable does such an excellent job at hiding that the son appears in the scene as the character of greatest importance. That is to say, the love of the father is so profound that he does not mind sharing the stage with his son.

The love of the father is so great that he is willing to place all the attention on his son so that his son would grow and succeed in doing things he never did. It is something very similar to what God the Father did when he sent His only son to be known as the Savior of the world, and as such, the central theme of the Bible is the salvation of humanity through a Redeemer, (Jesus, the Son) divinely chosen.

In this book, I want to share with you some truths that I found when I read this parable of the love of the father in Koine Greek.

When we study this parable in its original language, we can clearly see that there are five different perspectives of what a father is. Although there are five different perspectives presented in the parable, God wants to give us the correct perspective.

Alvin Toffler said, "The illiterate of the 21st century will not be those who cannot read and write, but those who cannot learn, unlearn, and relearn." For this reason, I want to invite you to explore with me in this book what is truly hidden inside the heart of the Father. I invite you to learn, unlearn, and relearn some very important things that will enrich your life.

I want to present to you the five perspectives that were found in the house of the father. These five perspectives are that of the older brother, the younger brother, the day laborer, the young servant, and the mature servant that worked in the father's house.

Chapter 7

The Different Perspectives in the Father's House

When we examine the history of what some translators have called "The Parable of the Prodigal Son" in the original Greek language, we learn that there is a distinction between the three servants that worked in the father's house. In this way, by studying the identity of each servant, we can understand that each had different perspectives with regard to what was the heart of the father.

When the King James Bible was written the translators apparently did not see the depth of the use of the different words in Greek to describe the three servants. It is for this reason that when you read this parable in the King James translation, you find the word "servant" to describe the three workers, which were different one from the other.

However, in the Spanish 1960 Reina Valera translation there was something interesting that the Spaniard translators were able to observe. They captured the distinction that Luke, as author of this Gospel, made between the three different types of servants. In this translation three different words are used to describe those that served in the father's house. The three names that are used are "day worker," "young servant," and "servant." Each of these workers have a different lens of paternity.

There are many factors that contribute to the different perspectives of a father. Many people have received a poor model in their childhood and adolescence of what a true father is–a father according to God's heart. These negative experiences in childhood and adolescence can contribute to a distorted lens of what paternity truly is according to the biblical model. For example, in the Bible we can see the case of King David, who was rejected by his biological father and even by his brothers.

God has created family as the first institution with the goal of validating his eternal purposes in the lives of our children. Even when many fathers fail, the Bible teaches us this lesson in Psalm 27:10, "Though my father and mother forsake me, the LORD will receive me." In other words, if the first institution created by God — that is, the family — fails in guiding and providing me with the resources that I need to have success in life, God will receive me.

The word that corresponds to "forsake" in Hebrew is "*azab*," which means "leave behind," "abandon." Now then, the Hebrew word for "receive" is the word *"acaph." Acaph* means to *pick up, be their rearguard and join.* That is to say, join together all the broken pieces that the wounds and the ill treatment created in such a way that our life now in God will be completely restored. The negative experiences in childhood can create a distorted perspective of what a father is according to the biblical model expressed in Luke chapter 15. Emotional wounds that have been caused by family tragedies can create a distorted paradigm or a fragmented lens of what the heart of the father looks like. A biblical example is that of Jonathan's son and grandson of King Saul, Mephibosheth. We find part of his story in 2 Samuel 4:4 which says, "Jonathan son of Saul had a son who was lame in both feet. He was five years old when the news about Saul and Jonathan came from Jezreel. His nurse picked him up and fled, but as she hurried to leave, he fell and became disabled. His name was Mephibosheth."

Mephibosheth is the classic example of a child whose perspective of a father was distorted. Mephibosheth had royal blood running through his veins; however, he was in the wrong location. Instead of being raised inside of the palace walls, he was living in a place called *Lo Debar. Lo Debar* was the name of a city that literally means "no pasture, no grass." The word "*lo*" in Hebrew means "no" and the word "*debar*" means "pasture."[1] "*Debar*" also comes from the Hebrew root that means "word." We could then say that this boy found himself in a place where there was no solid word for his life. If we choose to live in a place where there is no abundance of God's word, we can dry up and possibly never reach the destiny that God has reserved for our lives.

Lack of true identity is another cause that leads us to have a distorted vision of what God's paternity is. Mephibosheth was in a place where there was no word of God for his life. But thanks to the covenant that David had made with his father, Jonathan, David would send for him and help him in spite of Mephibosheth's resistance. David helped him to break the distorted paradigm of paternity. He brought him to the palace and sat him at the King's table where he was able to eat next to the King's children. There are many people who today are in the field or the city of *Lo Debar* because someone dropped them in their childhood, and they have yet to be able to embrace God's purpose which will lead them to God's destiny for their lives. In order for a person to be able to embrace all of God's purpose for their lives, it is necessary for them to know their identity and origin. If I am not able to understand why God placed me here on earth and what my design is, I will never be able to embrace His purpose for my life. Another factor that has contributed to distorted lenses of paternity is the absence of paternal father figures in our nation, even amongst God's people.

Chapter 8

The Younger Son's Perspective

Luke 15:11 tells us: "There was a man who had two sons. The younger one said to his father, 'Father, give me my share of the estate.' So he divided his property between them." Here we have a son who enjoyed the privilege of paternity and a home where all the characteristics of a tender and loving father were present. However, this son allowed rebellion to enter into him, and he was blinded from the correct perspective of the heart of the father. Possibly, bad company began to corrupt his character and distort his vision. It is obvious that his love for his father began to grow cold and that he lost the gratitude he once had for his father's provision. It is very probable that he became impatient with his father's governing style and leadership.

One day he began to demand that his father give him his inheritance. The Hebrew custom at that time was to give a son his inheritance when the father was dead; therefore, this rebellious son was wishing—in an indirect way—for the death of his own father. In Deuteronomy 21:18-21 the law informed fathers that rebellious sons had to be taken to the gates of the city to be stoned publicly. This was done as a testimony within the people of Israel with children that despised paternal authority.

In the Old Testament, God ordered Moses to stone every person that would not submit his life to the respective authority. If a man or woman committed the sin of adultery, for example, they were violating the authority of holy matrimony, for which they would be stoned. In the same manner, when a person rebelled against priestly authority, this was considered a violation of authority and that person would have to be stoned.

In the case of this rebellious son, under the principle of the law, statutes, and ordinances of the people of Israel, he was to be stoned. What Jesus' audience could not understand was the principle of grace in this story. They did not understand how it could be that instead of taking his rebellious son to the gates of the city to be stoned, he honored him by giving him his inheritance.

The story narrates that a few days after the young man had received his inheritance, he gathered all he had and set off for a distant country. There he squandered his wealth in wild living. This son's perspective of the father was based on individualism and rebellion. We could say that he represents many people that live inside the Church and due to external circumstances and peer pressure, reject the blessing of paternity and the honor of living in the Father's house. It is evident in the life of this young man that he left the house of the father before time.

This reminds me of many people that make decisions prematurely. Without exaggerating, I can affirm that this young man represents today's generation, the one many sociologists call *"The Y (Why) Generation"*. This generation questions everything. For example, if their parents send them to study, they want to know *"Why?"* The worst thing is that many of them—before they have developed emotionally, spiritually, and intellectually—think they know more than their parents. Many of them take on the attitude of the younger brother in the Parable of the Lost Son and want their parents to give them all the freedom possible to do as they please.

What many of these young people don't understand is that the majority of us do not develop, intellectually or emotionally, until approximately twenty-one years of age. According to many psychological studies, the prefrontal cortex of the human brain (which is majorly accredited for being responsible for judgment and reasoning) is the last part of the brain to develop. It is this part of the brain that allows adults to weigh their actions and the related consequences. It is also the part that helps us to resist peer pressure and stops us from doing foolish and ridiculous things that we may regret in the future. Many of these psychological studies have determined that the prefrontal cortex does not develop enough to make prudent decisions until the age of twenty-one. It is for this reason that the Apostle Paul says in Galatians 4:1-2, "What I am saying is that as long as an heir is underage, he is no different from a slave, although he owns the whole estate. The heir is subject to guardians and trustees until the time set by his father."

Paul understood that the practice of the tutors to look after the children was necessary due to the lack of maturity in the latter. The children were like slaves until the time the father determined that they had passed the test of maturity and then they would receive their inheritance. Although the younger son in the parable had not passed the test of maturity his father still gave him his inheritance. That was one of the reasons why Jesus' audience questioned the validity of his teaching on this matter.

The rebellion of a child, many times, is created by the lack of identity in life. Many children rebel because they have not learned to trust their parents. Others rebel because they allow external influences to create erroneous concepts of who they truly are. One of the consequences of leaving the house of the father before time is the squandering of all the talents, gifts and abilities.

One of the first experiences that I had with a rebellious child was when I was nineteen years old. At this time, I was living alone in the United States, since my parents had retired and were living in Puerto Rico. One day I received news about a young man I knew that had been kicked out of his home due to his rebellion and internal struggles. This young man was sixteen years old and was a son of a pastor that had experienced a lack of stability in his life due to several factors.

His father had been involved in ministry for more than two decades and boasted of being so "sensitive" to the voice of God that he had moved more than twenty times during his ministerial journey. This caused endless emotional problems in this young man. I was then moved to receive him in my home with his mother's permission, which asked me earnestly to do all that was possible to help him. When I unofficially "adopted" this young man, I received him into my home, helped him obtain a job and then I began to teach him about the grace and favor of God. In this manner, I established norms and rules in his life because he needed them in every area: emotional, spiritual, and intellectual. A few days later, he began to manifest his gratitude to God for all the good that was happening to him. I began to exercise my first "paternal" experience at nineteen years old by supervising an adolescent.

It goes without saying, that this young man had many limitations and had been hurt in his childhood and adolescence. I established a baseball system of three *"strikes"* and of strong norms with him, and in less than a week he had his first *"strike."* In a month, he had his second *"strike"* and each day that passed he was committing more mischief. After three months he did something very improper, dangerous and inappropriate, and I gave him the third *"strike."* I then decided to return him to his parents' home in Puerto Rico. I bought two airline tickets and asked an older friend (whose presence intimidated him greatly) to help me speak strongly to this young man so he would submit to our agreement. We had agreed that if he violated the norms, he authorized me to return him to his home, and now he did not want to honor the agreement.

The night of the confrontation, he simply refused to fulfill his commitment to me of returning to his parents' home. He threatened me and told me he would never allow me to send him back to Puerto Rico again. This situation became very difficult for me and for this reason, my friend and I had to watch him all night to make sure he didn't run away from the apartment. The next morning I went to the airport with him, my older brother and our pastor.

My pastor and older brother accompanied us until I was able to board the plane with him. Since we left our apartment that morning, that young man had not spoken a single word. He displayed an angry demeanor, showed frustration and rebellion. We managed to board the plane and he kept silent during the flight.

His countenance began to change after having been on board for two hours. He surprised me when he smiled and said; "You know that last night when you guys were watching me, you all fell asleep and I could have run away? The only reason why I did not run away was because I could feel that you love me. Since I know how much you love me, I decided not to run away, but honor our agreement of you returning me to my parents' home if I misbehaved." I began to smile and cry because we managed to establish a relationship where this young man could understand that he was loved very much, and that God certainly had a wonderful plan for him.

During the rest of the flight, we had a beautiful conversation about what the love of God does. I took him directly to his home in Puerto Rico and we managed, thanks to God, to reconcile this young man with his biological parents. We were able to succeed in leading him to adjust his distorted paternal lens and years later, we were able to see the results when this young man was able to get married and establish a solid home with a wonderful woman of God.

Instead of looking at his father as a hero, as his protector, as he who sacrificed everything so that he could enjoy many privileges, the son in the parable began to see his father as a figure that opposed his "success." In that same manner, the young man in my own experience was only able to understand his father's heart when he humbly returned to his home.

Chapter 9

The Older Son's Perspective

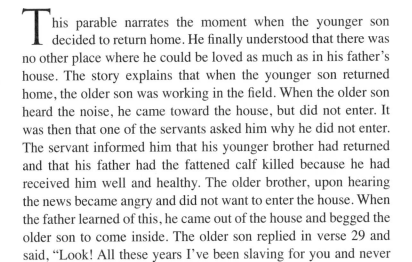

This parable narrates the moment when the younger son decided to return home. He finally understood that there was no other place where he could be loved as much as in his father's house. The story explains that when the younger son returned home, the older son was working in the field. When the older son heard the noise, he came toward the house, but did not enter. It was then that one of the servants asked him why he did not enter. The servant informed him that his younger brother had returned and that his father had the fattened calf killed because he had received him well and healthy. The older brother, upon hearing the news became angry and did not want to enter the house. When the father learned of this, he came out of the house and begged the older son to come inside. The older son replied in verse 29 and said, "Look! All these years I've been slaving for you and never disobeyed your orders. Yet you never gave me even a young goat so I could celebrate with my friends."

This older son suffered from an unhealthy syndrome of comparisons and of competition within his family. Sadly, there are many people who do not understand the heart of the father; they believe he has favorite children and that they are called to compete instead of complementing one another. The older son was envious and jealous, and for this reason could not enjoy the restoration of his brother. When the younger son had left the house, it appears that the older brother remained with a root of bitterness in his heart. According to the tradition of the time, a double portion of the father's inheritance was due to the first born. In this case, two thirds of all the inheritance belonged to him, because there were only two males. However, this older brother was so worried and focused in what was happening with his brother that he could not see the great blessing that God had for him.

I call this the "Peter Syndrome." The apostle Peter constantly compared himself with John. He continued to compare himself even after the death and resurrection of Jesus. In John 21:15, the Bible says that after he had eaten, Jesus confronted Simon Peter and asked him if he truly loved him more than the rest of the disciples. Jesus was asking Peter this question because he was comparing himself to John. Jesus wanted to establish a powerful principle of complementation in the Kingdom of God.

In the Kingdom of God we should not be comparing ourselves with anyone, because God is going to hold each of us accountable individually. One day we will be judged according to what God has called us to do with the gifts, talents, and abilities that he has given us in this life. Jesus finished confronting Peter and then he prophesied about how he was going to die in John 21:18, "Very truly I tell you, when you were younger you dressed yourself and went where you wanted; but when you are old you will stretch out your hands, and someone else will dress you and lead you where you do not want to go." Jesus said this to indicate the kind of death by which Peter would glorify God. Then he said to him, "Follow me!"

In other words, he was saying, "Peter, mind your business and worry about my holy calling for your life." Verse 20 tells us that turning, Peter saw that the disciple whom Jesus loved was following them, the same one that at the dinner had leaned back against him and had said, "Lord, who is going to betray you?" When Peter saw him, he said to Jesus: "Lord, what about him?" and Jesus answered: "If I want him to remain alive until I return, what is that to you? You must follow me."

In Luke 15:31, the father of the house tries to have the older brother not focus on the younger brother. The father says, "My son you are always with me, and everything I have is yours." In other words, "You have not only received a double portion of my inheritance, but all that is mine is yours." At the Father's house, there will be people that will not understand or embrace the grace of God because they are always going to embrace and prefer the law. The law stated that the first-born received two portions of the father's inheritance, but now under the covenant of grace we do not receive a double portion, instead we receive the whole inheritance. That is to say, all that the Father has is mine. That is why the Bible tells us in Romans 8:17, "Now if we are children, then we are heirs—heirs of God and co-heirs with Christ, if indeed we share in his sufferings in order that we may also share in his glory."

We are no longer simply those that have received a double portion, but we are those that have received all of the father's inheritance. Given that the older son had the mistaken perspective of the heart of the father, he could not embrace and rejoice in his father's grace. The son was embracing a promise, while the father was trying to connect him to the reality of grace. If there is something we need to learn as heirs of the New Covenant, it is that we are not people that simply have promises.

Hebrews 11 teaches us that all of the people that lived before the death and resurrection of Jesus Christ simply had promises. The patriarchs and heroes of the faith only had promises, but knew that only through the Messiah would all the promises of the Old Covenant be fulfilled. Now through the sacrifice and resurrection of Jesus Christ, you and I who are children of the New Covenant do not only have promises, but also have a complete inheritance. We are heirs and coheirs with Christ. There are people that do not live as God designed because they are still waiting on a promise, when the truth is that God has given us—as children of the Kingdom— keys, tools and treasures to live as children of the most high King.

When I was a boy, my mother would tell me the story of Goldilocks and the three bears. This was a story about three bears that cooked some succulent porridge. When the bears saw that the porridge was too hot, they went out for a walk in order to let it cool off. When they went out, they left the door open to their house. This is how a little intruder named Goldilocks entered into the bears' house, ate the little bear's porridge, sat on the smallest chair and broke it. She also lay on the little bear's bed and messed it up. When the bears returned to their house they were alarmed that someone had violated their privacy.

What we learn from this story is that when we leave the door to our house open, an intruder can arrive and sit in the place of authority God has destined for others. They can lay on the bed that God designed for us and dream the dreams of God that could elevate us to fulfill His plan and lead us to realize His destiny for our lives. They can also eat the food that God has designed for us to eat, simply because we were careless in securing and protecting our home.

There are people that go through life unsatisfied because they have not recognized who they are in Jesus Christ. It is for this reason that there are other people eating their food, dreaming what they should be dreaming and sitting in places of authority where they should be sitting. I encourage you to take your place and understand the heart of the Father that extends with grace and favor toward you. The older brother did not understand the value of what he had. He told his father that he had never given him a young goat, when in reality he had already received a double portion of the inheritance at the time that his younger brother received his share. The older brother's lens was damaged.

There was a moment in my life when my personal lens of the heart gave me a distorted view of the Father. When I began to pastor, my lens to see other people was a lens similar to the Pharisees in Matthew 23:25-26. "Woe to you, teachers of the law and Pharisees, you hypocrites! You clean the outside of the cup and dish, but inside they are full of greed and self-indulgence. Blind Pharisee! First clean the inside of the cup and dish, and then the outside also will be clean." I was examining the external things before examining the heart of man.

One day a young woman arrived to our congregation that God would use to transform my life forever. God used this young woman to repair my broken lens, which I thought was a lens with the correct perspective of the Father's heart. My lens was filled with traditions and dogmas, to such an extent that I could not see that my own heart was wounded and hurt.

This young woman arrived to our congregation and asked me for a time of counseling after a service. She was a little different than the other young women that I was pastoring at that time, with regards to her attire and external décor. Unfortunately I had been instructed and taught to judge the heart of a person based on how they were dressed, and so I sinned in exercising wrongful judgment.

When that young woman opened her mouth, she began to share how it was that in her childhood, a family member had sexually abused her. Then she continued to tell me about how it was that after some years, she was abused by a biological brother and years later it was no longer abuse, but through mutual accord she had become used to having intimate relations with him. She told me that through the years, she had lost a sense of value for her own body and she would enter into different relationships with young men, where they would periodically participate in sexual acts. Sex did not have much meaning for her. Through the years, her mother's female friend also abused her and she entered into a season of much confusion. She did not know if she was designed by God to have intimate relations with women or with men. Hearing her story, my heart began to break because she continued to tell me that in various occasions she had experienced abortion, and that she had also tried to commit suicide several times.

When I asked her to remain with us and allow us the privilege of helping her and completely restoring her, she sadly replied: "Pastor, you cannot accept me here because you are different, and I would never be accepted in a place like this." My eyes filled with tears and my heart trembled, because I knew the ecclesiastical roots of this young woman. I knew this young woman had grown up in a classical Pentecostal home, and that her parents had not noticed their own daughter's hellish journey.

The life and future of this young woman was in danger. Her heart was hurt and destroyed, and religion had not allowed me to see the depth of her wounds. That was the last day that I judged a person based on their wardrobe or external décor. I felt humiliated and like a failure. I felt I had offended the heart of God by not valuing human beings as God values them. That was the day that our ministry changed. It was when we began to understand the principles of Matthew 23–that God first cleanses the vessel inside, and then all the rest is realized by means of the work of the Holy Spirit.

We should not judge before we know the entire story. One of the things that we learn from the older son is that his perspective of the heart of the father was an erroneous one. The older brother thought that the father was being partial and did not value his efforts and all his contributions to the family. When the father shared with his older son about the restoration of his younger brother, the father could clearly see what was in his older son's heart.

Chapter 10

The Perspective of the Day Laborer – *"Misthios"*

There is a great difference between the three types of workers that served in the father's house. This is more noticeable when we study the parable in the Greek language called *"koine."* When we study the identity of each servant, we can understand that they each had different perspectives in regard to the father's heart.

Spanish translators caught the distinction that Luke made between the three different types of servants. In Luke 15:19, he uses the word *"misthios"* to describe a type of servant. A day laborer or *"misthios,"* is a servant that works for money. If there is a reward, he works. This servant works based only on profit.

This speaks to us about the perspective in the father's house that tries to earn or buy love and grace. In the father's house, love, favor, and even grace cannot be bought. God extends his love toward all of humanity and a father should extend his love toward his children without making any exceptions. However, the grace and favor of God as a Father cannot be bought. God gives a measure of grace to each person according to his desire.

The *"misthios"* is the person who does not understand grace, but thinks that everything in life has to be bought. This represents people within the family of God that do not work unless their actions bring forth benefits for them. A famous declaration made by the late president John F. Kennedy during one of his speeches was, "Ask not what your country can do for you — ask what you can do for your country."

We live surrounded by a culture that tells us, "Work according to what people can give you and according to what you can get out of them." This is the reason why inside the family of God, we find people that arrive or choose a place to congregate based on what the local church or ministry can offer them. Instead of looking at what they can contribute to help the Church of God advance and expand the Kingdom of God, they seek to be served.

The perspective then of the day worker is that of a consumer. In a sermon series that I often preach titled, "Consumers and Investors," I teach about the principles that God establishes in his word so that his children become investors and not consumers. The Bible teaches us in Isaiah 55:10 and 2 Corinthians 9:10 that God provides seed for the sower and bread for the eater. In other words, God gives bread to the consumer and seed to the investor.

> *"As the rain and the snow come down from heaven, and do not return to it without watering the earth and making it bud and flourish, so that it yields seed for the sower and bread for the eater"* (Isaiah 55:10).

> *"Now he who supplies seed to the sower and bread for food will also supply and increase your store of seed and will enlarge the harvest of your righteousness"* (2 Corinthians 9:10).

God desires much more for us than what we are living out in the "status quo". God desires to prosper us much more than we can imagine. Why should we settle for less? The Apostle Paul in his letter to the Ephesians addressed this issue. Ephesians 3:14 tells us, *"For this reason I kneel before the Father, from whom every family in heaven and on earth derives its name. I pray that out of his glorious riches he may strengthen you with power through his Spirit in your inner being, so that Christ may dwell in your hearts through faith. And I pray that you, being rooted and established in love, may have power, together with all the Lord's holy people, to grasp how wide and long and high and deep is the love of Christ, and to know this love that surpasses knowledge—that you may be filled to the measure of all the fullness of God. Now to him who is able to do immeasurably more than all we ask or imagine, according to his power that is at work within us, to him be glory in the church and in Christ Jesus throughout all generations, forever and ever! Amen."*

A few years ago the IRS reported that there were 1.8 million millionaires in the United States of America. Each year approximately one hundred thousand people become millionaires; in other words one every five minutes. Ninety percent of each of these people have worked hard with their talents, abilities, time, energy and discipline. Many of them simply have learned to value what is in other people.

According to Jacques Wiesel, "A poll of 100 independent millionaires showed one common factor, and that was that these highly successful men and women could only see the good in other people."[1] It is just not enough to work for oneself, but it is necessary to work for others and learn to seek the value that others have within themselves. Many people want a job that is above average, and they have not understood that to obtain a job that is above average, which pays above average, one has to be a person that is above average. One has to rise to the indicated level in order to qualify for that job.

In Matthew 25, we find the parable of talents and stewardship:

> *To one he gave five bags of gold, to another two bags, and to another one bag, each according to his ability. Then he went on his journey. The man who had received five bags of gold went at once and put his money to work and gained five bags more. So also, the one with two bags of gold gained two more. But the man who had received one bag went off, dug a hole in the ground and hid his master's money. After a long time the master of those servants returned and settled accounts with them. The man who had received five bags of gold brought*

*the other five. "Master," he said, "you entrusted
me with five bags of gold. See, I have gained five
more." His master replied, "Well done, good and
faithful servant! You have been faithful with a few
things; I will put you in charge of many things.
Come and share your master's happiness!" The
man with two bags of gold also came. "Master,"
he said, "you entrusted me with two bags of gold;
see, I have gained two more." His master replied,
"Well done, good and faithful servant! You have
been faithful with a few things; I will put you in
charge of many things. Come and share your master's happiness!" Then the man who had received
one bag of gold came. "Master," he said, "I knew
that you are a hard man, harvesting where you have
not sown and gathering where you have not scattered seed. So I was afraid and went out and hid
your gold in the ground. See, here is what belongs
to you." His master replied, "You wicked, lazy
servant! So you knew that I harvest where I have
not sown and gather where I have not scattered
seed? Well then, you should have put my money on
deposit with the bankers, so that when I returned I
would have received it back with interest. So take
the bag of gold from him and give it to the one who
has ten bags. For whoever has will be given more,
and they will have an abundance. Whoever does
not have, even what they have will be taken from
them. And throw that worthless servant outside,
into the darkness, where there will be weeping and
gnashing of teeth."*

This parable teaches us that a steward gave five talents to a servant, to another he gave two, and to another one, each according to
his capacity and then he went far away. God expects us to work and
produce at 100 percent of our capacity. In this parable's example, to
the one that was given five talents, it was expected that by working
at 100 percent of his capacity, he would produce another five. To

the one that received two, it was expected that by working at 100 percent of his capacity, he would produce another two. The one that received one talent, it was expected that by working at 100 percent of his capacity, he would produce another one, but it was not so. The one that had received five talents produced at 100 percent, and the one that was given two produced at 100 percent, and the one that was given one became afraid. He did not negotiate or invest his resources, and as a result he suffered severe consequences.

We are all called to be responsible and use each resource at our disposal in such a way that we can change our condition. Many times lack of growth has to do directly with attitude. I like the phrase that someone used in such an occasion when they said, "attitude determines altitude." The correct attitude will take you to a higher level. The *"misthios"* does not understand that even though we have to work hard to reach what God has determined that we achieve in life, we cannot buy his favor.

The *"misthios"* loves to work but if he does not get paid, he becomes angry, because he is seriously focused on money. He represents the type of person in the Kingdom that although he does not love money, he trusts and depends on it. The *"misthios"* are the same kind of people that do not understand how it is possible for the father to do what he pleases with what is his. These are the people that stumble with the parable of the workers in the vineyard. In Matthew 20:1-16, we find this beautiful parable:

> *For the kingdom of heaven is like a landowner who went out early in the morning to hire workers for his vineyard. He agreed to pay them a denarius for the day and sent them into his vineyard. About nine in the morning he went out and saw others standing in the marketplace doing nothing. He told them, "You also go and work in my vineyard, and I will pay you whatever is right." So they went. He went out again about noon and about three in the afternoon and did the same thing. About five in the afternoon he went out and found still others standing around. He asked them, "Why have you been standing here all day long doing nothing?"*

"Because no one has hired us," they answered. He said to them, "You also go and work in my vineyard." When evening came, the owner of the vineyard said to his foreman, "Call the workers and pay them their wages, beginning with the last ones hired and going on to the first." The workers who were hired about five in the afternoon came and each received a denarius. So when those came who were hired first, they expected to receive more. But each one of them also received a denarius. When they received it, they began to grumble against the landowner. "These who were hired last worked only one hour," they said, "and you have made them equal to us who have borne the burden of the work and the heat of the day." But he answered one of them, "I am not being unfair to you, friend. Didn't you agree to work for a denarius? Take your pay and go. I want to give the one who was hired last the same as I gave you. Don't I have the right to do what I want with my own money? Or are you envious because I am generous?" So the last will be first, and the first will be last.

It is interesting to see how the influence of our western culture affects our attitude with regard to the blessings that others experience. In the East, people put more emphasis in collective success, but in the West we put more emphasis on the individual's success. This spirit affects the Church in a negative way. It is for this reason that instead of becoming joyful with the extraordinary progress of a new minister or congregation, some of us resent it.

This is exactly what happened in the parable found in Matthew 20. Some got angry because other workers had a shorter work shift and received the same compensation. Instead of being happy for the blessing of their co-workers, they were overcome by envy and jealousy. God desires to take us to a level where we celebrate the success and accomplishments of one another instead of feeling intimidated and insecure about the successes of others. The *"misthios"* is bothered when someone is paid more than him. This type of perspective in the house of the Father is that of a person that puts a price on ministry and other things. Instead of allowing it to be the Father who determines the compensation, they go ahead and put a price on the labor for the Father.

Chapter 11

The Perspective
of the Young Servant – *"Pais"*

I n Luke 15:25, we read that when the older son was in the field
and heard the music and dancing, he called one of the servants.
In verse 26, the Greek word for servant is *"pais."* A *"pais"* is used
to describe a very young servant. It is the same word that is used in
the Greek to describe a child. The *"pais"* represents he or she that
has an immature perspective with regard to the heart of the father.

This represents people that have not yet developed the ability
to discern the heart of the Father, and for this reason they often
misinterpret His motivation. People with this perspective exist in
every congregation, and sadly they do not have a clear context or
a better definition with regard to the heart of God. They are people
that draw conclusions without first having all the necessary elements to have or hold a just trial.

The evidence of this can be found right in verse 27, when
the older brother asked the servant, in other words the *"pais,"*
"What was going on?" The *"pais"* informed him, "Your brother
has come and your father has killed the fattened calf because he
has him back safe and sound." This was not the truth. The reason
the father killed the fattened calf was definitely not because he
received the son well and healthy. Absolutely not!

We read in Luke 25:27 that the father celebrated because, "this
son of mine was dead and is alive again; he was lost and is found."

In verse 32, it is also emphasized: "But we had to celebrate and be glad, because this brother of yours was dead and is alive again; he was lost and is found." The *"pais"* misinformed the older brother because of his immaturity. In the body of Christ, there will always be immature people. These are the kind of people that focus on the glory of a ministry without the process. They have the tendency to desire glorious results without a Calvary type of experience.

Because this immature person has not developed the capacity to examine things well, he or she will always walk with the wrong perspective. The *"pais"* is that person that does not understand that the human being sees things not necessarily as they are, but according to how he or she is. The *"pais"* thinks he is mature, when in reality, he still has a long way to grow.

Paul gives us a good example of this in 1 Timothy 3:6, by using the word *"neofite"* to describe an immature person. A *"neofite"* is a new convert resembling a plant that has recently emerged or been born. These type of people want to embrace greatness without being processed and without first having paid the price of experience.

The *"pais"* is also a person that due to his or her immaturity sows discord in the body of Christ. In verse 27, we see that because the young servant misinformed, the older brother became angry and refused to go into the party. While it is very true that the older brother had deeper personal issues than the misinformation received from the *"pais,"* the truth is that the *"pais"* provoked a situation and worsened it.

The *"pais"* also represents people that do not understand and do not have the heart to get involved in the conflict resolution of biblical restoration according to Matthew 18. These are the kind of people that when the father of the house needs to bring restoration, they tend to judge things without understanding. They are lovers of the law and lack grace and mercy.

Chapter 12

The Perspective
of the Servant *"Doulos"*

I n Luke 15:20-24, we find the verses that capture the return of the younger son to the father's house. He decided to return and choose the way of repentance. When the son returned to the house, the father sent his servants to restore him. In verse 22, the Greek word for servant is *"doulos"*. The *"doulos"* is the servant that understands the grace, love, and forgiveness that resonates in the heart of the father.

The *"doulos"* represents the trusted servant, that is to say the mature servant. The *"doulos"* speaks of that person that has been able to understand a measure of the grace of God. These are people that have experienced the power of God's forgiveness in their lives, in such a way that they utilize meekness as a means to consider others with regard to restoration. When these kind of people hear about another person's tragedy, their hearts tremble because they are filled with Godly compassion, mercy and forgiveness. These are people whose hands are filled with balm to bring healing to the broken hearted. These are the kind of people that when they hear news of a fallen soldier in the army of Christ, instead of taking a stone into their hands and throwing it, they are the first in dropping the stone and asking that God also have mercy on them. These are people that understand and live out the Bible verse that says, "So, if you think you are standing firm, be careful that you don't fall!" (1 Corinthians 10:12).

The heart of the *"doulos"* speaks of a heart that has learned to pay a price in life. It's the manifestation of one that has been processed in life and that has created his ministry out of his pain and misery. For this reason the father of the house delivered his younger son to the *"doulos"* – so that it would be the *"doulos"* who would be in charge of his restoration. Allow me for a moment to use my imagination, and think about the possible process or the possible journey of this *"doulos."* I invite you to enter with me for a moment in the world of the servants of that time:

"Hello, my name is Doulos and I am a slave. Did you know there are various types of slaves and that not all of us are the same? There are people that are slaves due to war and are sold as a result of their army losing the battle. There are others that are slaves because they did not manage their finances well, and now as a consequence of bad stewardship, they are forced to sell themselves as slaves with the goal of paying their debts. I am not a slave due to war or as a result of my debts, but I am a voluntary slave. I delivered myself voluntarily to my master as a slave, however it was not always this way. I was born into slavery, but I want to share with you some of my story.

I never had a father when I was growing up. I never knew what it was to experience the love of a father. I was separated from my father when I was born, then from my mother when I was twelve years old. I was sold at an auction, "a discount" people would say to me, and that truly affected and hurt my self-esteem until the day that I found something powerful in this house. My desire is that you may also find it, because what I found in this house changed my life forever. Allow me to tell you more of my story.

At the age of eighteen, I ran away from the house that I had been sold to the first time, and when they found me they returned me to the house and gave me such a lashing that they almost killed me. This created in me a rebellious spirit and for this reason, I refused to work with all my might in that house until they sold me. They sold me to this house where I am now. When I arrived here I discovered that there were two children—two heirs—an older

83

brother and a younger brother. At first, I was under the impression that they were good boys, but something strange happened.

Understand something, the father of this house, in other words the man who all call father, is very different from the master I had in the past. This father showed me love and affection, and for this reason I suspected that there was something wrong with him. I thought that he must want something from me. How could it be possible that a master take interest in a slave? How could it be possible that a master show so much love? Then the unexpected took place.

One day I entered into a depression so great that it caused a revolution in my mind. I decided to run away again. One night I escaped and ran so far that I thought they would never capture me. This time it was different. They captured me and returned me to this house. This master did not do what my first master did. He did not punish me, did not mistreat me, but he brought me to his house and showed me love. He embraced me and brought correction to my life. I could not understand why he did not mistreat me. I simply could not understand it.

The other servants had told me to look for something exceptional in the house that could change my life forever. I had never looked for it until this day. My life was transformed because my master validated me. He found in me the value that no one had given me.

I remember that one day, the younger son of the house rose and asked his father for his inheritance. The time had not come for this son to receive his inheritance. His father was still alive. He had not died, he was not even sick. However, his younger son demanded his inheritance and his father was so good and loving that even though his rebellious son was asking that he die, he took the inheritance and gave it to him. I could not understand it. How could it be that this son, instead of being stoned by the father of the house, is being blessed? But then things got worse.

After a few weeks, the son said to the father, "Father, it's time for me to leave this house. I no longer want to be here. I want my own house, want my own things and want to be my own boss." When I heard the words of the son I thought the father was going to take him to the gates of the city, because the law says that rebellious children must be stoned. But something amazing happened.

The father hugged him and said, "Son, this is your house, you belong to this house, and there's no need for you to leave this place. If this is what you want to do, I want you to understand something, and that is that in this house there is a lot of love for you and my desire is that you never leave. If you decide to leave, I want you to know that the moment you decide to return, I will receive you with my arms open because I love you."

At that moment, the father kissed him and hugged him, and later his son left. That was the day my life was transformed as a slave. After I fulfilled the years the law required of me as a slave, I refused to leave my master's house because I understood that leaving that house, I would never be able to find the paternal covering that this father had given me.

In this house I found my purpose. I am on my way to my destiny, because in this place I encountered the heart of the father. With this father I learned to put others in first place, instead of myself. With this father I gained the confidence to serve. With this father I learned to take the initiative to be able to serve others. In this house I have come to understand that what matters most is not a position, but rather to exercise a function with the goal of serving others. And in this house I have learned to serve, not considering what is given to me, but instead motivated by the love the father has extended toward me and the love I have decided to give him in return.

This is the reason I surrendered myself voluntarily to him after my time of required slavery was completed. I went with my master to the gates of the city and declared publicly: "I will not leave you, because I love you and I love your house, and because things go very well for me when I'm with you." Before the elders of the city and all witnesses present, my master took an awl and pierced my ear against the gate of the city, and declared publicly, "You will be my servant forever," and I replied, "Amen.""

Very well, let us return to our previous perspective. The Apostle Paul in his epistles applies the Greek term *"doulos"* to describe a man or a woman that give themselves to Jesus voluntarily as slaves to righteousness. Romans 6:18 says that we have been "set free from sin and have become slaves to righteousness." In Romans 6:22, the apostle Paul says, "But now that you have been set free from sin and have become slaves of God, the benefit you reap leads to holiness, and the result is eternal life." In other words, when a person really knows the heart of the Father, he is ready, just like the *"doulos"* in the parable of Lucas chapter 15, to give himself voluntarily to the service of the Father because of love and love alone.

Chapter 13

Validation

E very child needs validation. Some need it more than others, but all need a dose of validation. The younger son of the parable in Luke 15 returned home repentant because he had a great need to be affirmed. In Luke 15:22, the father said to his servants, "Bring forth the best robe, and put it on him." The first thing the father did was call his *"doulos"* or servants. The original language says he called the *"doulos."* Why didn't he call the *"misthios"* or day laborers? He did not call the *"misthios"* because they did not understand the grace and mercy of the father.

If he would have employed the services of the "misthios" to restore his son, they would not have worked with the best attitude, because they would have restored the younger son through the mindset of doing only those things for which they would be compensated. This represents people in the Church that restore with interest. Many times people come into conflict when they need to restore a person that owes them something. Many times they lack the heart of God and the understanding of the majestic union between mercy and God's justice. This union took place in Christ Jesus and happened on the Cross of Calvary.

Why would it be that the father of the house did not call the *"pais"* or young servant to restore his younger son? The reason he did not call the *"pais"* is because the *"pais"* did not have the experience and least of all the maturity to restore the younger son. The "*pais*" possibly would have demoralized him, for he did not have the correct perspective of the heart of the father. For this reason the "*pais*" wrongfully informed the older brother that was in the field, with regard to what truly motivated the father of the house to kill the fattened calf.

The father of the family called the "*doulos*" because he had the correct perspective of what the heart of the father is. The first thing the father did was give the "*doulos*" the instruction of restoring the identity of his son. Why? Because every child needs validation. The reason why there is an increase of violence in our culture and an increase in gang recruitment in our nation is because many of these young people are looking for someone to affirm them. These young people are looking for validation! If the biological or adoptive fathers don't affirm them, and if we as a church do not take our place in affirming these children, then the curse that the prophet Malachi spoke about will come. Destruction will come over our families and gangs will win the battle. The father said, "Bring forth the best robe." In other words he was saying, "This is my beloved son in whom I have contentment, because even though he does not deserve to be called my son, he has arrived at my house with a contrite and humble heart and a genuine spirit of repentance. I forgive him and I validate his identity. This is my son."

That father restores the identity of his son and tells his servants, those that have the heart of "*doulos*," (a heart ready to restore), "Bring the best robe and put it on him. Put a ring on his finger." There he restores his authority using a robe and ring as symbols of his position and function. Then he places sandals on his feet, and validates his identity because slaves did not use sandals in those days. Finally the father says, "Bring the fattened calf and kill it. Let's have a feast and celebrate. For this son of mine was dead and is alive again; he was lost and is found.' So they began to celebrate."

As a result of the poor models of paternity that many of us have had, there exists a multitude of children waiting to be validated. The reason there is so much competition amongst the people of God is because there is a cry and clamor of children seeking paternity and asking that someone please recognize that they are important, that they are called by God and that they have a very important role or function to carry out in the Kingdom of God.

We are living in a prophetic season when we need to pour ourselves out completely into the next generation. We need to wake up and be sensitive to the cry of ministerial orphanhood. We need to hear the clamor of an Elisha that cries out in a loud voice, "My father! My father! The chariots and horsemen of Israel!" (2 Kings 2:12). I have to declare with much respect that paternity is not provided by means of a theological school or ecclesiastic structure. In the days of Elijah and Elisha there were schools for prophets. There was a school for prophets in Gilgal, another in Bethel, and another in Jericho. Nevertheless, there was an absence of a paternal figure in the lives of these prophets.

For this reason, when the mantle of paternity fell upon the prophet Elisha, the prophets of all the schools were always following him, because in him they found something that the schools could not give. What was it they were seeking? They were in pursuit of the mantle of paternity. Paternity transcends denominations, movements, councils, apostolic networks and any type of religious structure. Paternity is not a man-made structure. Paternity is a relationship.

Paternity is lived through relationships that are obtained in the Kingdom of God. There are many young people that today walk around confused without knowing what to do with their lives due to an identity crisis. What led the younger son in the parable of Luke 15 to leave his house was simply an identity crisis. If you ask a newly graduated college student today, "What do you want to do with your degree?" It is very likely that he or she will reply, "I am keeping all of my viable options open." In other words, "I still don't know what to do with my life." When a person understands paternity, they can understand the importance of validating children and providing them with direction.

Conclusion

Saving and Restoring What Had Been Lost

I n the Gospel of Luke, we learned that when the younger son asked for his inheritance prematurely, the father of the house blessed him. Instead of cursing him, dishonoring him, and applying the law to him, he honored his son. The law required that the father take him to the gates of the city and stone him along with the elders of the city due to his rebellion. But the father used his blessing as a door to give this son grace, favor and mercy even though he did not deserve it. Paternity blesses even when a son deserves to be cursed. Let us look at Luke 15:17-20, which says:

> *When he came to his senses, he said, 'How many of my father's hired servants have food to spare, and here I am starving to death! I will set out and go back to my father and say to him: Father, I have sinned against heaven and against you. I am no longer worthy to be called your son; make me like one of your hired servants.' So he got up and went to his father. But while he was still a long way off, his father saw him and was filled with compassion for him….*

I want to point out the fact that verse 17 states that the son came to his senses. In other words, while the son was lost and walking in disorder, his father was interceding for him, so that all the powers of darkness, which were binding his mind would release him. The father prayed and interceded for his son, so that he would embrace God's purpose. Verse 20 indicates that even while he was still far away, his father saw him. This means that the father loved him so much, that despite his rebellion, the father knew that one day his son would return home. For that reason, it is very possible that the father waited every day at the city gates with the purpose of preserving his life. The father knew that according to the law, his rebellious son would be stoned the moment he arrived at the city. Deuteronomy 21:18-21 tells us:

> *If someone has a stubborn and rebellious son who does not obey his father and mother and will not listen to them when they discipline him, his father and mother shall take hold of him and bring him to the elders at the gate of his town. They shall say to the elders, "This son of ours is stubborn and rebellious. He will not obey us. He is a glutton and a drunkard. Then all the men of his town are to stone him to death. You must purge the evil from among you. All Israel will hear of it and be afraid."*

This is the reason why the father waited for him at the city gates every day, because he wanted to save the life of his son. The father knew that the moment his son chose to return, it would be due to a repentant heart–a heart that supernaturally was going to return to the heart of the father. That is why even while he was far away, the father saw him, was filled with compassion and ran to him.

We understand that the audience to which Jesus was telling this parable must have felt completely perplexed and probably asked themselves, "How is it possible that a father run to a rebellious son when in our custom rebellious sons are the ones that have to run to their fathers due to their shame?" Jesus, once again, was using hyperbole as a tool to shift paradigms of men. He was using this parable as an example of the powerful love that God the Father has for all of humanity.

God loves us so much, that even when we have sinned and we do not deserve to be forgiven, He forgives us. What we deserve is death due to our sin, but the heart of God the Father leans toward us. This way, when we are repentant, he runs toward us. The father ran toward his rebellious son because he had repented with all his heart.

When the father reached him, he threw his arms around him and kissed him. The son quickly said, "Father, I have sinned against heaven and against you. I am no longer worthy to be called your son." The father listened to him and understood perfectly what was happening on the scene: his son had repented with all his heart. When there is genuine repentance, there exists *a yielding and surrendering of all our rights*. When a person truly repents, he does not defend himself, does not justify, or enter into arguments or reasoning with regard to reasons why sin was committed.

Sin is not something someone falls into; instead it is something that a person decides to do. In 1 Corinthians 10:13 we read these words, "No temptation has overtaken you except what is common to mankind. And God is faithful; he will not let you be tempted beyond what you can bear. But when you are tempted, he will also provide a way out so that you can endure it."

This biblical verse indicates clearly that a person does not fall into sin, but that they choose to sin because they ignore the warning of the Holy Spirit that guarantees to always give us a way out so that we can withstand and defeat all temptation.

One of the key elements needed for a process of effective restoration is that the person that has committed a sin demonstrate a spirit of genuine repentance. The younger son of this house surrendered all his rights as a son. When he said to his father, "I am no longer worthy of being called your son," the father understood what the son was trying to indicate. The son was trying to indicate, "Father, I have failed you, but I desire that even if it is as a worker or a hired servant, you allow me to enjoy your covering." One of the most important things that we must understand is that the Kingdom of God is established upon relationships. Therefore, the most important thing in the Kingdom of God is not properties or material things, but relationships. This repentant son was able to understand that the most important thing in the father's house was not the assets, but the relationship and covering that the father offered.

He said, "Father, I am no longer worthy to be your son or to carry the name of this house, but please allow me the privilege of being like one of your hired servants because even the servants have an abundance of bread in your house." In other words, he was telling the father of the house, "I am no longer interested in the tangible things or what you can give me. I am no longer interested in your properties and resources, instead all I simply want is to embrace your paternity. I want your relationship; I want to have the relationship of a son with you, even if it is as a servant."

When this younger son came to his senses, he was able to understand how much love, favor, grace, mercy and forgiveness was found in his father's house. For the older brother, the father's action toward the younger son was truly surprising because his theological framework informed him that an ungrateful son was treated with beatings and iron rods. He did not understand why it was that the father did not receive the younger son citing Psalm 1:1 which says, "Blessed is the one who does not walk in step with the wicked or stand in the way that sinners take or sit in the company of mockers."

He was not able to understand how it was that his father covered his brother with love instead of allowing his rebellious brother to enter the city as he had left it, so that he could be stoned to death. The older son could not understand why his father said, "My son was dead and is alive again; he was lost and is found." He did not understand that this declaration restored his younger brother and allowed him the privilege to enter through the city gates as a new man, and in this manner avoid the curse that corresponded to him, death.

Some Lessons and Principles of Restoration:

- The true condition of humanity is revealed in these parables.
- God's mission is evident and is manifested – to save the lost.

- God's compassion and love point out to us the price He paid.
- God and the Church work together to restore.
- Restoration is a celebration.
- The character of many is proven in the restoration process.

The Process of Restoration:

- The sinner is lost.
- The sinner is valued (someone has to pay the price).
- Someone prays and intercedes for the sinner.
- The sinner is searched for.
- The sinner is found or located.
- The sinner is saved.
- The sinner is restored.
- The sinner is delivered and his salvation and restoration is celebrated.

The Sinner is Valued

Each city is filled with gold even if it appears to be the poorest city in the world. The Bible establishes in Proverbs 13:23 that the fallow ground of the poor would yield much food, but it is swept away through injustice. Each person has value, no matter how deep they are submerged in sin. Each person has unlimited value. When a person or congregation understands the value of the human being, an awakening is experienced regardless of whether it is an individual, nation, or continent because the power of value restores anyone.

The younger son was rescued because his father learned to value him even when he was submerged in sin. One of the secrets to the success of the church I pastor, The Cityline Church, is that we have learned to see God's value in people that are marginalized and rejected by our society. In 1 Samuel 22:1-2, we find the writings concerning David's 400 men, "David departed from there and escaped to the cave of Adullam. And when his brothers and all his father's house heard it, they went down there to him. And everyone who was in distress, and everyone who was in debt, and everyone who was bitter in soul, gathered to him. And he became commander over them. And there were with him about four hundred men."

In other words David had to see what the glory of God was in these men. The glory of God is the intrinsic value that God places in us. Paul called this value a treasure, the treasure of Jesus Christ, "But we have this treasure in jars of clay, to show that the surpassing power belongs to God and not to us..." (2 Corinthians 4:7).

Paul also declares that in Christ Jesus are hidden all the treasures of the wisdom and intelligence of God. He admonishes the Colossians to reach all of the riches of complete understanding of God, with the goal of knowing Him more.

"I want you to know how hard I am contending for you and for those at Laodicea, and for all who have not met me personally. My goal is that they may be encouraged in heart and united in love, so that they may have the full riches of complete understanding, in order that they may know the mystery of God, namely, Christ, in whom are hidden all the treasures of wisdom and knowledge" (Colossians 2:1-3). Therefore, if we want to build something great for God, we have to begin to value the people that are most despised by society, for God can do anything, at any time, when a person has a willing heart.

These 400 men that came to David were afflicted and indebted in bitterness of spirit, but were restored because the anointing that was in David was poured over them. As a result their affliction was removed, their debt was cancelled and the bitterness of spirit was eliminated because they were able to receive what was in David.

As a minister, I have learned to see the glory and the value of God in broken and marginalized men and women in society. In 1996, God challenged me to move the location of the congregation I was pastoring to one of the worst communities in all of the United States of America. The place was called Curries Woods. More than twenty five years ago, when I was living in my native city of New York, I watched *ABC News Nightline* with Ted Koppel. I will never forget one of the interviews he did, which marked my life and my heart forever. He found himself in Curries Woods–a community of public housing where there were seven tall buildings for poor folk (commonly referred to as housing projects). Ted Koppel was interviewing the drug addicts in that community as they injected themselves with drugs. That was something beyond belief! More astonishing was the fact that less than ten years later God would call me to pastor a congregation and buy a property in the midst of that same community.

In 1996, I fell in love with that disenfranchised, despised and rejected community–Curries Woods, in Jersey City, New Jersey. We found a property that was on sale in the same heart of this community and we covered it with prayer. We believed God for a miracle and in 1997, we already had the keys to the property closest to these housing projects. God had given us a word that He would transform all of this community, and in a few years we saw how God began to fulfill His word.

A year after we moved to our new location, the federal government granted our municipality a housing grant of more than $32 million to demolish six of the seven skyscrapers. They were going to build town houses for the residents, which would be able to rent their new houses with option of purchasing them.

We have seen a complete transformation in our community because we believed that a depreciated territory contained much worth. God has given us the privilege of receiving men and women that arrived afflicted, indebted, and with bitterness in their spirit. Notwithstanding, today they are men and women that have been healed, prospered, manage ministries, own businesses and are free of all affliction. These are people that have experienced the joy and blessings of God at an extraordinary level.

Love Languages

In his book, *The Five Love Languages*, Gary Chapman presents us with the idea that every human being has a love language that is their primary language. Chapman presents the love languages as: words of affirmation, acts of service, quality time, receiving gifts, and physical touch or affection[1]. In Luke 15, when the younger son returned to the Father's house, he was received with much love. The father of the house exemplified all of the love languages that Gary Chapman presents in his book.

The father showed *affection* running toward his son, hugging him and kissing him despite the disgraceful condition in which his son found himself. The father understood what the younger son told him about not being worthy to be called his son and insinuated that he be received as a laborer. However his father insisted in restoring him and called him "son." In other words, the father used *words of affirmation* to validate his hurt son. The father also displayed *quality time* by going to the city gates every day, waiting for his son to return home one day. The father invested much time in his son.

The father also showed *acts of service* by preparing a great feast for his younger son, celebrating his symbolic death and resurrection, killing a calf and throwing a great party. Lastly, the father also demonstrated the language of *gifts* by sending his servants to dress his son with the best robe, putting sandals or footwear on his feet, and also honoring him with a ring of authority. As fathers, it is important to learn and recognize the love languages of our biological and spiritual children. This will enable us to guide them in the path and in the purposes of God for their lives. Each child has a primary love language and knowing the language will allow us to be of greater blessing for that son or daughter.

My Father, My Father: A Cry of Orphanhood

In the year 2004, my biological father was diagnosed with cancer and I could never imagine how much I would miss him. But when God decided to call my "old man" home to be in His presence, I was able to experience in my life the cry of Elisha when he exclaimed, "My father, my father." My father was a pillar in the house of God. He was not a pastor, but he walked the streets seven days a week serving in ministry.

He was the person responsible for managing and driving the church van that our congregation primarily used to pick up families that did not have the means to get to the church facilities. My father was also one of the people that opened and closed the congregation's facilities. He loved God with all his heart. He was my hero in life. He taught me what it truly was to serve God will all integrity and all honesty.

My father became an orphan while only in the third grade and for that reason he had to leave behind his academic studies at a very young age. He had to begin to work to support himself and his younger brother. My father did not have the opportunity to study or prepare himself academically at an advanced level, but was a brilliant man and learned to work with his hands and back. We never lacked bread in my house. He learned to give us love through providing for us. He was not an extremely affectionate man, due to the lack of tenderness in his childhood as a result of his parents' absence, but he did show us to love God with all our hearts, and above all to have fear of God. When there is a fear of God in the life of a man or woman, there is reverence and respect for the things of God. There is a respect so sacred for the things of God, that when a person sins, he not only confesses his sin and departs from it, but also renders an account to others.

When there is no fear of God but there is fear of man, the tendency of the human being is to sin and sin until he or she sinks deeply. One of the things that we learn from the parable in Luke 15 is the abundance of grace and forgiveness that existed in the father's house. There will always be grateful sons and ungrateful sons in the father's house. The older son showed his lack of gratitude even when the father begged him to please enter the feast and join him in celebrating the restoration of his younger brother.

In the Kingdom of God there will always be men and women that act without shame and that do not deserve the father's grace and favor. Sometimes the love of the father is so great, that it covers them with grace and favor even though they do not deserve it. This was the attitude of King David, when he abandoned his throne because of his son Absalom. Absalom had been disloyal and had divided his father's kingdom, yet his father king David, loved him so much that he left his palace with the goal of saving his son's life.

When a person understands true paternity, many times he will take great and serious risks, where he places his own reputation in danger with the goal of saving the life of his children. As the lead pastor of the Cityline Church for over twenty three years, I have had the experience of blessing and restoring children that left our congregation saying things that affected our image as ministers. I have learned throughout the years that sometimes it is better to not defend yourself or dishonor these children publicly–instead leave the door open so that at the time of repentance, they can return home and still be restored. If you exercise paternity, many times the people closest to you will be the ones responsible for the deepest wounds in your heart. When a person understands paternity, he or she can live the principle that Paul shared with the people in Romans 12:19-21 which states:

> *Do not take revenge, my dear friends, but leave*
> *room for God's wrath, for it is written:"It is mine*
> *to avenge; I will repay," says the Lord. On the*
> *contrary: If your enemy is hungry, feed him; if he*
> *is thirsty, give him something to drink. In doing*
> *this, you will heap burning coals on his head.*
> *Do not be overcome by evil, but overcome evil*
> *with good.*

I learned this principle with one of my older brothers, when I saw him go through an unjust ministerial situation. At times I wanted to defend him and many times I tried, but he remained in silence and never defended himself. Today I understand that God was using him to give me an example of what it means to not be overcome by evil, but overcome evil with good.

Through my paternal journey in these two decades, I have learned to bless even those that curse me. I have learned to love unconditionally. When a person is willing to love unconditionally, he or she will always be at risk of being hurt. The wounds have been many, but they cannot be compared with the lives that I have seen come to the feet of Jesus and experience not just salvation, but the holy calling to ministry. The declaration of the father in the parable, "For this son of mine was dead and is alive again; he was lost and is found," is a prophetic declaration of what happens in the life of a man when he dies to the things of the past and together with Christ is crucified and resurrected. That is why the father saved him outside the city, just like Jesus Christ, the Son of God and the savior of the world gave his life for me and was crucified outside of the city of Jerusalem.

Appendix

Succession Planning

Every wise father leaves an inheritance and a powerful legacy to his children. We are taught in Proverbs 13:22 that a good man leaves an inheritance to his children's children or the future generations. The heart of God as a Father is a heart that thinks in terms of generations. Thinking in terms of generations is visualizing succession planning.

The book of Ruth narrates a powerful story of succession planning that starts with a family that entered into crisis due to a famine. One of the things that we should remember is that through human history, God has used famine as a time of testing when paternity is healed and restored. For that reason, Ruth 1:1 begins with these words.

> *In the days when the judges ruled, there was a famine in the land. So a man from Bethlehem in Judah, together with his wife and two sons, went to live for a while in the country of Moab. The man's name was Elimelek, his wife's name was Naomi, and the names of his two sons were Mahlon and Kilion. They were Ephrathites from Bethlehem, Judah. And they went to Moab and lived there. Now Elimelek, Naomi's husband, died, and she was left with her two sons. They*

married Moabite women, one named Orpah and the other Ruth. After they had lived there about ten years, both Mahlon and Kilion also died, and Naomi was left without her two sons and her husband. When Naomi heard in Moab that the LORD had come to the aid of his people by providing food for them, she and her daughters-in-law prepared to return home from there.

Historically we are living in a time where God desires to restore paternity and above all, to help us exercise healthy succession planning. What is succession planning? Succession planning is the ability to raise and lead our children strategically, in such a way that God's purpose for their lives will be fulfilled. Succession planning is also the skill to strategically launch our children like arrows that will change the course of history for good. Psalm 127:1-5 tells us:

Unless the LORD builds the house, the builders labor in vain. Unless the LORD watches over the city, the guards stand watch in vain. In vain you rise early and stay up late, toiling for food to eat— for he grants sleep to those he loves. Children are a heritage from the LORD, offspring a reward from him. Like arrows in the hands of a warrior are children born in one's youth. Blessed is the man whose quiver is full of them. They will not be put to shame when they contend with their opponents in court.

Succession planning is also exercising the ability to train, equip and disciple our children in such a way that the Kingdom of God is established here on earth. In Psalm 127, Salomon declares that what makes a city strong is that God has established it and that God is guarding it. In this Psalm, the principle that children are like arrows in the hands of a warrior is established. In other words, our children have been designed by God to be equipped, trained and discipled in our homes and ministries so that the purpose of God is fulfilled in them.

It is important to recognize that God desires to perpetuate the purpose that He deposited in us through our seed – our children. Therefore, God has called us to transcend what is our own generation, imparting to the next generation gifts, talents, abilities and equipping it in such a way that they do greater things than we did in the expansion of the Kingdom of God.

The book of Ruth begins with an interesting scene, where we are informed that the judges were ruling. The Bible says, "In those days Israel had no king; everyone did as they saw fit." There was an absence of paternity and one of the reasons for which there existed an absence of paternity was due to Joshua. Joshua had been a tremendous leader that was able to introduce the nation of Israel into what was the Promised Land. However, when Joshua died, the people of God fell into chaos and disorder.

Joshua had failed in *succession planning*. Joshua represents ministers that leave nothing behind to keep the ministry alive. When they die, their whole ministry is buried with them because they did not prepare the next generation to continue what God had given to them. It is for this reason that the book of Judges begins with chaos. When paternity is absent, we can expect chaos, disorder and lack of direction.

When a famine arrived in the land, according to the book of Ruth, Elimelek did not exercise paternity according to God's model; instead he opted to run away in the midst of the crisis. Elimelek lived in a place called Bethlehem, Judah, in other words he lived in a state called *Praise* and in a city called *House of Bread*. It is possible to live in a place whose name represents purpose and destiny and yet not understand God's process. This can cause many people to run away from growth opportunities that God puts before them.

It is for this reason, that in the midst of this paternity famine we must avoid running to what appears to be the best place for ministry. Instead of doing that, we must embrace the desert where God sends us to build a ministry because when it is God that calls us and sends us, He will always make manna descend from heaven and fresh water come out of a rock in the midst of that desert.

Elimelek ran away and a few years later he died because he left the land of praise and the house of bread and ran away to the valley in Moab. In the Bible, Moab represents the place where visions die and where dreams are buried. Moab is the place where frustrated ministers end up, just like Moses, who due to disobedience refused to change his ministerial paradigm and philosophy. This resulted in God laying him to rest permanently in Moab.

We need to honor our leaders from the past, but we also need to learn from the mistakes of past generations so that we never repeat them. Apparently, Elimelek cursed his children Mahlon and Kilion with the names he gave them. Their names mean "sickly" and "weakling." We need to do things in a different way. It is important that the names and words we declare over our biological and spiritual children be names of purpose and destiny. At this hour we have to build a generation that understands their purpose, their identity, and their destiny with clarity.

Elimelek deviated because he did not understand his purpose, and even less his identity. For that reason, Elimelek never developed his potential. What is potential? Potential is reserved power, your unexercised skills, it is success that is inside oneself, but that is yet to be utilized. It is the gifts and talents that are already inside, but that are still hidden.[1] It is what you can reach and have not reached, it is all you could see, that you have not yet seen.

This is a time when we need to take the knowledge of the truth of God to this new generation so that the truth will set them free. John 8:32 says, "Then you will know the truth, and the truth will set you free." It is important to note here that what makes us free is not the truth, but the *knowledge* of the truth, because when a person comprehends the truth, he is able to break the molds and all limits that detain him.

A New Vocabulary

In order to exercise healthy succession planning it is necessary to develop in this new generation a new vocabulary and a new way of thinking, given that a new vocabulary and way of thinking will give us a new life. This is why the Proverbs 23:7 (NKJV) states, "That as a person thinks in his heart, so is he." We have to learn, unlearn, and relearn many things. One of the things that we have to teach this new generation is a new language that does not use words to oppress or to keep ethnic groups, races, nations, and entire continents bound.

I give God thanks for the privilege of having been born in the United States. This is a blessed nation; a nation that God desires to lift to a higher level. This is a nation that God desires to heal in such a way that we can continue to advance in what is our progress of equality by giving all that arrive an opportunity to grow and prosper. However, we have a long way to go, and it is necessary to instruct people to embrace their identity in Jesus and transcend human concepts designed to bind their progress.

We have to teach this new generation that there is no such thing as a third world country, but that the phrase "third world" is still used by many to mentally and emotionally enslave and oppress the nations of the Earth. We live in one world and because we live in one world, there cannot be a third world. When we think we form part of a *third world*, we will never form part of the first and only world. If we believe a lie, that lie can become our reality.

It is time to end with the lies and embrace the knowledge of the truth of the Word of God. African Americans, Latinos, and people of other ethnicities are no longer minority groups in this nation. The word "minority" was designed to oppress people in the United States. For many years this word was used to describe ethnic groups in relation to population, but in the last several years Latinos are among the groups that have advanced rapidly in relation to population.

It is interesting that the *centers of power* and the *dominant culture* continue describing the Latino group as a minority group. Now they have changed the definition again in such a way that a minority group is no longer a classification with regards to population. It has been redefined in order to put a stigma of contempt on our Latino community.

When many Europeans arrived at the United States, they were called "explorers" and the history books in our public schools still describe them as such. However today when people come from other countries seeking a better opportunity to live in what is a better socio-economic environment, we do not call them explorers. Now we call them "illegal." Even when many immigrants have the appropriate documentation and are legal residents on their way to becoming citizens, we give them an identification called the Resident Alien Card.

We have to end this oppressive language that has the specific intent of emotionally binding the success of many people. We have to change our archaic and limited vocabulary and way of thinking. Sometimes, leaders of the most prosperous international nations abuse others, using a certain type of language. For example, some of the people that live in the United States call themselves "American," but truly those of us who live in the United States are not the only Americans. Those that live in countries in Central America are also Americans, and those that live in South America are as well. What has happened is that those of us that live in the United States have taken ownership of the term "American" and we sometimes look down on others that do not live in our great nation.

Another thing that we need to teach our children is that the first people to arrive to this land were not the English with Sir Walter Raleigh from Great Britain when he came to Virginia. Nineteen years before Sir Walter Raleigh arrived to Virginia, the Spanish that were in Cuba arrived in Florida and founded what today is known as Saint Augustine, the oldest city in all of the United States of America.[2]

It is important to also teach our children that twelve years before the first Pilgrims arrived at *Plymouth Rock*, the Spanish had already founded what was the city of Santa Fe in the state of New Mexico in the United States.[3] We have to teach our children and this next generation that we are called to bless and love all that God blesses and all that God loves.

God loves the immigrant in such a way that Jesus was born in Asia, and at the appointed time was sent to Africa (Egypt) and lived as an African refugee until the fulfillment of God's word arrived, when he returned to Asia. Jeremiah 29:11 says, "For I know the plans I have for you," declares the LORD, "plans to prosper you and not to harm you, plans to give you hope and a future." God desires to prosper people from every nation, tribe, tongue, and people group.

God loves all of humanity and desires to see the continuous development of his people in the entire world. Currently I am working on a doctorate in Global Leadership and because I feel a burden in the area of succession planning, I have decided to possibly do my dissertation on this theme. I have already begun to write on this with the purpose of using it to finish my next book. I am studying to be able to offer solutions on "How to Develop and Implement Effective Succession Planning." I have begun to identify the obstacles that prevent a congregation from being able to continue growing and taking the influence and culture of the Kingdom of God to society. Not much has been written on this theme, therefore we need to identify the causes and offer solutions. Some of the possible causes are the lack of education, poor financial planning, insecurity, and erroneous theological concepts. I am already working to offer practical and effective solutions.

We must continue to learn and for that reason one of my goals as a father and leader is to be a life-long professional student. Tony Campolo tells in his book, *Who Switched the Price Tags* that there was a poll done of a sociological study of fifty people that were older than 95.[4] In the poll they were asked: "If you could live life all over again, what would you do differently?" As you can imagine, there were all types of answers, but there were three that stood out and continued to resonate throughout the poll.

First, many said, "If I could live my life all over again, I would take more time to reflect." Others said, "If I could live my life all over again, I would take more risks." Others also said, "If I could live my life all over again, I would do more things that would live on even after I die." In other words, "I would leave a more powerful legacy." May God allow us to have such a paternal heart that even after we are gone, we leave a powerful legacy that continues to transform future generations.

NOTES

Chapter 1

1 Joan Berlin Kelly, *"Surviving the Breakup."*

2-6 1988 Census *"Child Support and Alimony: 1989 Series"* P-60, No. 173 p.6-7, and *"U.S. General Accounting Office Report"* GAO/HRD-92-39FS January 1992

7 U.S. D.H.H.S Bureau of the Census

8-9 Centers for Disease Control

10 *Criminal Justice and Behavior*, Vol. 14 p. 403-26

11 National Principals Association (*Report on the State of High Schools*)

12 U.S. Dept. of Justice, Special Report, Sept., 1988

13 Fulton County Georgia Jail Populations and Texas Dept. of Corrections, 1992.

14 US News and World Report, February 27, 1995, p.39

15 *Current Populations Reports*, US Bureau of the Census, Series P-20, No. 458, 1991

16 *Current Populations Reports*, US Bureau of the Census, Series P-20, No. 458, 1991

17-26 ***"Marriage: The Safest Place for Women and Children"***, by Patrick F. Fagan and Kirk A. Johnson, Ph.D. Backgrounder #1535.

Chapter 2

1 John Maxwell's teaching "The Law of the Price Tag."

Chapter 7
[1] W.E. Vine, *Expository Dictionary of New Testament Words*, vol. 3, pg. 158

Chapter 10
[1] John C. Maxwell, "Relationships 101" (Nashville, Tennessee— Thomas Nelson 2003, page 37)

Conclusion
[1] Gary Chapman, "The Five Love Languages" (Chicago, Il— Northfield Publishing, page 15)

Appendix
[1] Myles Munroe, "Understanding your Potential" (Shippensburg, PA—Destiny Image Publishers, page 21
[2-3] Justo Gonzalez, "Mañana" (Nashville—Abingdon Press, page 31)
[4] Tony Campolo, "Who Switched the Price Tags?" (Dallas, London, Sydney, Singapore—WORD 1986, pages 28-29)

About the Author –

Joshua Rodríguez

Joshua serves as the Lead Pastor at the Cityline Church, one of the fastest growing bilingual ministries in the Northeast of the United States. The Cityline Church is a congregation of more than 1,600 members in Jersey City, and is represented by over forty ethnic groups. Their weekly television broadcast airs in over 100 cities and towns throughout New Jersey, reaching more than one million households. Pastor Joshua founded a private Christian School for grades K-8, as well as planted a Church in Gibraltar, Europe. His ministry philosophy entails empowering people through the restoration of God-given identity, so that they positively impact every segment of society.

After enjoying a lucrative ten-year Wall Street career in Investment Management, Pastor Joshua resigned in 1996 to enter ministry full time in order to improve the quality of life of the people of Hudson County and beyond. In 2006, Joshua was appointed as the first Hispanic Police Chaplain of the 177-year old Jersey City Police Department. Pastor Joshua has had the pleasure of serving on several Governors' Transition Teams. He was a member of the Governor's Hispanic Advisory Council for Policy Development, and the Equal Employment Opportunity Commission of the State of New Jersey. He also served former Governor Jon Corzine as part of a Financial Literacy Task Force and as part of a statewide Latino Task Force, which provided strategic input, and planning related to the needs of the Latino community. Governors, Senators, Congressmen, Assemblymen, Mayors and various organizations in the Greater New York area have recognized his leadership.

Joshua is the Vice-President of NaLEC (The National Latino Evangelical Coalition), an advocacy group that focuses on improving the quality of life of all people by addressing key national and global issues such as poverty, immigration, and education. In 2009, he was awarded "Alumnus of the Year" from the Alliance Theological Seminary as a result of his leadership and outstanding ministry. In August of 2010, during the 50th Anniversary celebration of the "Jersey City Puerto Rican Heritage Festival and Parade," Joshua was recognized as "Puerto Rican of the Year." He is a leader that has been called to empower people and bridge the gap between generations.

Pastor Joshua holds a Bachelor of Science degree in Organizational Management from Nyack College, and graduated with honors from the Alliance Theological Seminary with a Masters of Divinity degree. Joshua was elected to "Who's Who Among Students in American Universities & Colleges" due to his outstanding graduate work. He was also elected to the *Omicron-Psi* National Honor Society.

He is currently working toward his Doctoral degree in Global Leadership. He is a dynamic and energetic speaker who has inspired and empowered people in many nations of the world including engagements in Argentina, Brazil, Chile, Colombia, Costa Rica, Cuba, Dominican Republic, Ecuador, Ghana, Gibraltar, Guatemala, Holland, Honduras, Italy, Mexico, Morocco, Panama, Puerto Rico, Spain, the United States, and Venezuela, as well as many others. Joshua and his wife Paula have four children and live in New Jersey.

Product Information

Quantity Purchases
Churches, bookstores, and other organizations may qualify for special terms when ordering quantities of this book.

For more information or to order, contact:
The Cityline Church
1510 John F. Kennedy Boulevard
Jersey City, NJ 07305
Phone: 201-332-0970
Email: info@thecitylinechurch.org

For more information about engaging Pastor Joshua for keynotes, workshops, training and consulting, contact:
The Cityline Church
Phone: 201-332-0970
Email: info@thecitylinechurch.org
Website: www.thecitylinechurch.org
www.joshuarodriguez.info
www.theheartofthefather.com